HIGH SCHOOL THEATRE LIGHTING FOR ARCHITECTS

DESIGNING BACKWARDS

Elizabeth Bracken Rand

© Elizabeth Bracken Rand, 2015

TABLE OF CONTENTS

INTRODUCTION   6
       Jo the LD
       Designing the Lighting System to Design the Lighting
       About the Author

PART 1 – THE FUNDAMENTALS

1. THEATRE BASICS   11
       Who's Who Behind the Scenes
       Stage Directions

2. STAGE LIGHTING THEORY   15
       McCandless
       Intensity
       Distribution
       Color
       Movement
       McCandless' Light Plot
       Beam Angles and Field Angles
       Calculating Beam Angles

3. A LITTLE LIGHT PRACTICE   28
       Why is Light Important?
       Activities
       Results and Reasons

4. EQUIPMENT   39
       Instruments
       A Lamp, by Any Other Name
       Which Light Board?
       Light Board Placement

5. LEDs AND MOVING LIGHTS   45
       LED Cyc Lights
       Moving Lights

6. A SYSTEM FOR ALL   47
       Rep Plot
       Cheat Sheet
       Subs

7. TECH REHEARSALS   50
       The Start of the Show
       Concerts/Speakers
       Variety Shows and Dance Recitals
       Full Length Plays and Musicals
       Hanging and Focusing the Lights

        Tech Week
        Dry Tech
        The Design Process
        Theory to Reality

8.   LET'S BEGIN DESIGNING A LIGHTING SYSTEM 60
        Lighting Positions
        How Many Circuits
        Numbering Circuits

9.   TIPS FOR DESIGNING BLACK BOX THEATRES 68

PART 2: OTHER STUFF YOU SHOULD KNOW

10. WORK LIGHTS   70
        The Trouble Is…
        Why LED Work Lights
        Work Lights Policy

11. HEADSETS   75
        How Many Headset Jacks and Where
        Other Headset Positions to Consider
        Daisy-Chaining
        Wired vs. Wireless
        Batteries
        Single Channel vs. Double Channel
        Single Muff vs. Double Muff
        Muff Comfort
        Call Light

12. THE COUNTERWEIGHT SYSTEM   83
        Training
        Safe Operations
        Rigging
        Weights
        Lockout Tagout Tags
        Counterweight System vs. Electric Winch System
        Inspection

13. LIGHTING MAINTENANCE   93
        Work Parties
        Sample Summer Work Party To Do Lists
        Off Season Maintenance
        Perpetual Maintenance

14. STORAGE   97

PART 3 WHAT'S IT ALL FOR?

    15. STAGE LIGHTING EDUCATION   102
          Real World Applications
          In Demand Job Skills
          STTEM
          Learning Goals
          CTE – Vocational Education
          Technicians as Mentors
          Tech Theatre and Academic Success

FINALE

    16. BLACKOUT   118

    GLOSSARY OF TERMS   120

INTRODUCTION

JO THE LD

Jo is a lighting designer who has been hired to design the lights for a production at a high school theatre. She will be working with a five-person student lighting crew. One will run the light board, two will run followspots and two will be gel changers. When Jo arrived at the theatre it was to find cables strung back and forth between the catwalks hanging over the audiences heads, and the director complaining to her that the actors' faces were too shadowy – *I can't see their eyes!* – and could Jo fix that. The director also complained that set and costume colors looked dull under the stage lights. When Jo turned on the light board she discovered that the theatre had been operating on a one-to-one patch for two years because that's how the installers had left the system and the drama teacher didn't know otherwise. On top of that the acting teacher and the students had hung lights willy nilly, trying to cover up a dark spot here and a dark spot there, so that there was no functional rep plot. Nor had they gelled the lights, except for a blue wash. When Jo went to work with the students to create a rep plot, she discovered that there was the wrong number of the wrong type of instruments in the theatre's inventory to enable her to create a standard McCandless rep plot.

After further assessing the situation, Jo discovered that the reason the cables were strung across the catwalks was because there were only 10 circuits on the second beam – the beam from which two zones of area lighting and three color washes were typically hung. She also discovered that the reason the actors' faces, the eyes in particular, were too shadowy, was because the catwalks weren't installed in the right places to create a 45-degree lighting angle. She also discovered that there was one student, who was also a member of the school's robotics club, who had figured out how to control the lights on the light board in a rudimentary way, but the acting teacher and the other students did not know how to use it at all. When she saw the light board, she knew why. The light board was a new top industry light board with all the bells and whistles. It cost the school district a fortune and did far more than the lighting package required, and far more than a high school lighting system was capable of.

Jo also discovered some dangerous circumstances, including old lighting instruments stored in the catwalks without safety cables, and lighting cables strung across the catwalk decks without being gaff taped down – a major tripping hazard 30' in the air.

Jo's situation is not unusual.

These days there seems to be an insurgence to build state-of-the-art Performing Arts Centers (theatres) on high school campuses. Because of this trend more and more architects who normally specialize in designing schools are being thrown into designing theatres too.

DESIGNING THE LIGHTING SYSTEM TO DESIGN THE LIGHTING

Architects also find themselves appointed to design the stage lighting systems in the theatres. Having to design a theatrical lighting system without having an understanding of how the lighting needs to function is like being charged with painting the lines on a football field without knowing how the game is played. How can you be expected to design a theatrical lighting system if you've never "played" behind the scenes before?

In your personal life you go to restaurants, hotels, shopping malls, doctor's offices, perhaps even hospitals. You've cooked in your own kitchen and possibly run your own office. In your younger years you may have had a job in one of these facilities, and you've certainly set foot in schools. For the most part, you know how the lighting in these types of facilities should function, as enough of the "behind the scenes" operations are apparent and common knowledge. However, when you go to see a play, ballet, concert, opera or other performance, what has been going on and what is going on behind the scenes is not at all apparent. In addition, most of the lighting instruments are hidden from the audience's view, so all you see is the magic of the finished lighting design. And if it's designed well, you may not even consciously notice that either.

Because theatrical lighting is such a specialty architects, contractors or school districts will sometimes hire "lighting designer/consultants" to design their theatre's stage lighting system. But even this is not a panacea, because many companies that offer theatrical lighting consulting today are operated by people with no practical and functional experience designing stage lighting. In fact, a lot are from the home theatre or places of worship industries. Or, they worked in the theatre a long time ago, started their company, and haven't worked in the theatre since. Many of them have no practical or current experience in stage lighting. If you look at the websites of many theatre consultants, you will see that they are system designers and equipment installers with a wide range of experience working in churches, halls and home theatres. This does not necessarily indicate that they also have the specialized knowledge to properly design a live theatrical lighting system appropriate to its specific functions, let alone one specialized for a high school situation. In addition, school districts and other organizations – to their long-term detriment - usually go with the lowest bidder, who tends to be the one who will bid any job, and therefore is the one with the most generalized knowledge.

There are bona fide lighting designer/consultants out there. Be sure that any lighting designer/consultant you work with is a member of at least one of the following organizations:

ASTC - American Society of Theatre Consultants
IALD – International Association of Lighting Designers
IES – Illuminating Engineering Society

Within those organizations, look for people who are theatrical lighting specialists who periodically work in the theatre setting and don't just sit at a desk all day. Also look for lighting specialists who specialize in live performance venues.

If you personally don't have a practical working knowledge specifically in theatrical lighting, it's nearly impossible to anticipate what today's end user may need in terms of functionality. There's no better way to understand stage lighting than to go and work on a show at your local high school or community theatre. Unfortunately that's not an option for many busy architects. So this book will 'virtually' put you in the mind of a lighting designer, so that you can learn how the lighting is designed and then in turn design the lighting system to fulfill the functions needed. In short, we will start in the theatre and end at your CAD file. I call this process:

Designing Backwards

We must Design Backwards because the type of equipment installed directly affects building functionality, student learning and faculty retention. I've seen too many extravagant high school theatre stage lighting systems go to complete waste and not be used to their full potential because the design was not suitable to the users' abilities or budget. For instance, one school I worked at had a (mega overkill, ultra expensive) state-of-the-art light board installed with a complete system of programmable LED lights in their 100-seat theatre. I suspect the architect was concerned about energy and environmental design, and rightly so, but there are exemptions for performance spaces regarding energy consumption. The system was so complicated that no one had used the theatre's lighting system for the first year and a half of the school's operation. For a start, all of the lights had been left programmed to come on when the board was turned on and no one knew how to turn off the stage lights. They didn't know that the lights had been programmed into a cue. They didn't even know what a cue was. So my techs and I re-hung, re-focused and re-patched the lights (some which had even been left aimed at the wall outside of the proscenium arch, others right on the drapes). We then programmed the whole system for them in a rep plot format. That system will never be used to its full potential in such a preliminary learning environment and cost the school district hundreds of thousands of dollars. This is a classic example of where simpler technology (a "two scene preset" manual board with standard manually focused instruments) trumps state-of-the-art technology when it comes to building performance affecting academic performance, as well as assists with staff ability and retention of knowledge.

Without a background in stage lighting it is of course impossible to plan for every eventuality and for you to catch everything a theatre person would (even with a stage lighting background there is no way to plan for every eventuality!). But, reading this book and learning about the end functions of stage lighting, will help determine the initial design decisions you make, and help avoid the types of the issues Jo found in the opening vignette. You'll learn where to place electrics and how many circuits to provide, what lighting instruments to spec, what type of light board the situation requires, and lots more. More importantly this book will show you the "why". Why do catwalks need to be placed at 45 degrees? Why is state-of-the-art not always the best choice? Why do I need to spec this number of these instruments? When you know the why, then you will know the what, and you'll be Designing Backwards.

ABOUT THE AUTHOR

But, wait, before you go on, you are probably wondering who am I to write such a book. To rephrase a quote from Henry David Thoreau:

"How vain it is to sit down to write when you have not been up a genie lift!"

I am a Lighting Designer by training and trade. I began my stage lighting training at my own high school theatre in the years of dead-front light boards run by four technicians and manually operated carbon arc followspots. I was lucky enough to go to a high school that had a 950-seat performing arts center that was rented to outside events as well as being used for school productions (it still is). Students from the high school were paid to work under the leadership of professional technicians for plays, musicals, operas, movies, lectures and so on.

I started designing lighting professionally since the early 80's, but then moved to high school theatres. I have designed, or mentored student designers in over 100 school shows. I have worked in over 20 theatres (most of them schools). For several years I also worked as an architectural lighting designer; my singular claim to fame being the landscape lighting design package for the Hyatt Regency in Guam.

My undergraduate degree is in Drama; emphasis Stage Lighting, and my master's degree is in Entertainment Business Management. I also hold a Theatre Arts teacher certification. I was the Lighting Director for a production that won the "Rookie Event of the Year Award" at the Key Arena in Seattle, Washington, and I have been nominated three times for Best Lighting Design at Seattle's 5th Avenue Theatre's High School Musical Theatre Awards. My website address is:

www.RandConsultingandDesign.com

PART 1

THE FUNDAMENTALS

CHAPTER 1

THEATRE BASICS

WHO'S WHO BEHIND THE SCENES

Before you can begin to design a stage lighting system you should have a general knowledge of who are all the players the lighting designer works with. Below is a list of Who's Who Behind the Scenes. Not every school production or event will need every person on this list, and large productions will need all of them and more.

DIRECTOR - directs the actors in the show – in a high school this is usually the Drama teacher or a guest director, sometimes students assistant-direct full length shows or direct One Act plays.

CHOREOGRAPHER - choreographs any dance pieces in the show – this can be a teacher within the school (some sports teachers also know dance), a hired choreographer from a local dance company, or a particularly talented student.

MUSICAL DIRECTOR - works with the actors on any vocal pieces in the show, and/or rehearses and conducts the orchestra or band that plays with the show. There can be a vocal director and an instrumental director, or one person who does both. Again, a teacher (the school's choir and/or band teacher for instance), a hired musician from the community, or a particularly talented student.

STAGE MANAGER (SM) - assists the director at rehearsals, runs the show every night, calls all the cues, in charge back stage. In high schools, this is usually a student. Once the curtain goes up on opening night the student Stage Manager is fully in charge.

ASSISTANT STAGE MANAGER (ASM) - assists the Stage Manager, sometimes is in charge of props. Sometimes also known as the Deck Manager - if the SM is calling the show from the booth the ASM will be in charge of what goes on on the stage deck.

PROPERTY MASTER/MISTRESS (PROPS) – procures or creates the props (any object used by the actors which is not permanently built into the set), sets out the props used by the actors every night, makes repairs as necessary.

SET DESIGNER - designs the scenery, oversees the construction of the set pieces. In high school theatre this can often be a well-meaning parent who has usually had some construction experience, or a certificated vocational tech theatre teacher.

SET CREW - builds the set, usually the student and/or parents in a high school situation.

RIGGING/STAGE CREW – usually students who move the set pieces and scenery during a high school show, professional technicians for outside events.

COSTUME DESIGNER - designs the costumes, oversees the making of the costumes, makes repairs as necessary. In high school theatre this can often be a creative parent who has sewing and design experience, sometimes a professional from the community, or a certificated vocational tech theatre teacher.

COSTUME CREW - sews the costumes, usually the students and/or parents.

DRESSERS - help the actors with any quick or complicated costume changes during the show.

MAKE-UP ARTIST - designs the make-up, may help with application of complicated make-up. Usually students or parent volunteers take on this role for shows with more complicated make-up. If not, each actor is responsible for his or her own make-up.

LIGHTING DESIGNER - designs the light plot, oversees the hang and focus, attends tech rehearsals and decides on light levels to be set throughout the play. This is a specialty area, not usually found from within the school, like construction or sewing, so usually a Lighting Designer is often hired from the community, but can be a theatre technician employee who performs this task, or a certificated vocational tech theatre teacher who has a background in stage lighting.

LIGHT BOARD OPERATOR - programs the light board for tech rehearsals and runs the light board for the performances. Usually a student with a strong interest in, and aptitude for, lighting.

MASTER ELECTRICIAN - leads the hang, focus and patch, is the technician or student who is most familiar with the craft. The Master Electrician can also be the Light Board Operator but not always.

ELECTRICIANS or LIGHT TECHNICIANS - help with hang and focus, assists the Master Electrician if needed during the show, such as for gel changes, re-patching, helping execute a particularly complex manual cue on the light board, etc.

SOUND DESIGNER - designs the sound cues, oversees placement of mics on stage and/or on actors, attends Tech Rehearsals and decides on sound levels to be set. Light stage lighting this is a specialty area, not usually found in the outside world like construction or sewing, so usually a Sound Designer/Engineer is hired from the community, or can be a theatre technician employee who performs this task, or an experienced certificated vocational tech theatre teacher.

SOUND BOARD OPERATOR - programs the sound board for tech rehearsals and runs the sound board for the performances. Usually a student with a strong interest in, and aptitude for, sound.

MIC WRANGLER – in charge of helping the actors put their headset mics on backstage before and during a performance. Usually a student in the high school setting.

RIGGER – when hanging scenery or drops *ALWAYS* have the processed supervised by a qualified rigger. Remember that you are hanging hundreds of pounds of weight overhead. The correct hardware and process must be used. *NEVER* allow students to rig sets unattended.

RUNNING CREW – the people who move the sets and fly the scenery, during a show. Usually a team of students, ideally supervised by a theatre technician.

THEATRE MANAGER – the person who schedules events into the theatre, schedules the technicians needed to run the events, and works towards the success of each individual event. The Theatre Manager differs from a Stage Manager in that the Stage Manager manages an individual show that comes into the theatre, whereas the Theatre Manager manages all of the shows that come into a theatre. Because so many high school theatres operate as road houses (school, district and outside events) it is becoming increasingly common for high schools to hire a professional Theatre Manager and professional technicians to work with their students and supervise all of the events. This is a good Risk Management decision on the part of school districts. For more information about High School Theatre Operations Management, please see my book of the same name, which can be found on Amazon.

STAGE DIRECTIONS

As well as knowing who's who backstage you will also need to know where's where. At the end of this book is an extensive glossary of predominantly used theatre terms, but one of the important concepts you will need to know and will use a lot is stage directions. Here's a diagram.

```
                         STAGE DIRECTIONS

        Stage Directions are always from the actors' perspective.
                                                           BS
        SL    Stage left             / USR    US    USL \
        SR    Stage right           /                    \
        DS    Down stage           /  SR     CS     SL   \
        US    Up stage            /                       \
        DSL   Down stage left, etc. /  DSR   DS    DSL   \
        CS    Center stage        ----------------------------
        BS    Back stage
        FOH   Front of house                 FOH
```

Stage directions are taken from the actor's point of view while standing on the stage. So, if you are sitting in the house - stage left is to your right and stage right is to your left. However, if you are referring to something in the house, then you can refer to house left and house right, which are your left and right. When talking to someone on stage or about something on stage however, we always refer to stage left and stage right, even if you are sitting in the house.

You may understand the importance of always referring to the actor's point of view when giving directions or making reference to their left or their right, however you may be wondering which is down stage and which is up stage. Here is a history lesson that will help you remember.

In our day and age usually the stage is a flat horizontal surface and the seats in the house are set on an incline, or "raked". In Shakespearean times this was not the case. There were no seats in the middle of the house and those who could not afford the box/balcony positions that were around the edge of the house would stand on the house floor. However, because they were standing on a level surface it was hard for those in the back to see the actors on the stage. Therefore, stages in Shakespearian times were raked – sloped down towards the audience. So when an actor moved away from the audience he literally walked up hill, hence up stage being at the back of the stage, and when an actor moved towards the audience he literally walked down hill, hence down stage being at the front of the stage.

CHAPTER 2

STAGE LIGHTING THEORY

The theatrical discipline the majority of non-theatre people know the least about is that of Stage Lighting. Most people have had some experience in sound; playing, recording, adjusting the treble and base, etc. Most people have also had some experience in construction; for instance, as a child my father helped me build a swing, and in high school I took Art Metal Work. Some people have even made their own clothes, or at least sewn on a button. Of course, there's far more to theatrical sound, set building and costuming than that, but these topics don't seem to instill the trepidation factor like lighting design does. Short of installing a dimmer switch in their home, most people have little practical experience about the theory and practice of lighting design.

Before you can make decisions on where to place your catwalks, how many circuits you need, how many instruments you need to spec, and what is the best light board for the job, you need to walk backwards and ask what do theatrical lighting designers know about stage lighting theory that guides their decisions, and in turn will guide your decisions.

MCCANDLESS

In 1932 Stanley McCandless published a book titled "A Method of Lighting the Stage". Notice he didn't say "the" method, but just "a" method. However for many decades this has actually been *the* primary method taught in schools and used in the industry. These days we also have Broadway Lighting and other methods, but the McCandless Method is still the best starting point for learning about stage lighting. I recommend getting yourself a copy of this book if you can (it's out of print, but you can still find copies from the link on the Books page at www.RandConsultingandDesign.com).

Stanley McCandless taught many of the early greats of stage lighting, including Jean Rosenthal (also a recommended reading link found on the Books page, her book: "The Magic of Light"). My university stage lighting professor, Tom Ruzika, had the opportunity to meet and was inspired by Jean Rosenthal early on in his prolific stage and architectural lighting career (www.ruzika.com). So I consider Stanley McCandless to be my Great-Lighting-Grandfather.

THE FOUR PROPERTIES OF LIGHT

McCandless determined that there are four properties of light that can be manipulated to create mood and location, or to draw the audience's attention. The Four Properties of Light are Intensity, Distribution, Color, and Movement.

INTENSITY

Intensity is how bright the light is. The most important job of the lighting designer is to make sure the audience can see what's going on on the stage.

Some things to remember:

Intensity is relative.
For example, a single candle on a dark stage will appear bright, but a single candle on a fully lit stage would be hardly noticeable. (Not that you'd allow an open flame in a theatre…).

Intensity is adaptive.
The eye will adapt to a level of brightness and perceive it as normal, until the next cue. For example, a scene with all channels set at a level of 70% will seem bright after a scene with all channels set at 40%, but that same scene set a 70% will be perceived as dim after a scene with all channels set at 100%.

Mood is associated with intensity.
For example, bright light makes an audience more alert, and is more conducive to comedy, while a low light intensity can suggest a somber or scary mood.

The eye is drawn to the brightest part of the stage.
The brightest part of the stage can be determined by the reflective quality of an object. For instance, a single actor wearing a white costume among actors wearing colored costumes can be a walking bright spot.
Alternately, attention can be directed by the relative intensity of the light itself. The eye can be subtly drawn to an actor or area by increased intensity.

DISTRIBUTION

Distribution refers to both the angle the light is aimed at, and also whether the focus is diffused or sharp.

MOTIVATING LIGHT

When a lighting designer analyzes a script and prepares their design they must consider the motivating light. In other words, what motivates the direction the light comes from? Are there any light sources used on stage such as a table lamp or fireplace? Is there a light source out of sight such as sunlight, moonlight or the light from a hallway spilling through a doorway into a room? Through the distribution of light coming from the light source, the lighting designer can suggest that light is coming from that source by placing instruments above or behind the source to light the actor or the set from that direction.

The light may also be diffuse or sharp. For instance, sunlight is sharper – it casts defined shadows – while moonlight is more diffuse and soft.

The distribution of light is used for three primary purposes; lighting the actors, lighting the set, and effect lighting (setting mood, location, etc). Following are some tips for each purpose.

LIGHTING THE ACTORS

> AREA LIGHTING - Actors or dancers should be lit from two lights from the front at 45 degrees. One side is a cool (bluish) light and the other is a warm (pinkish) light. This mimics the psychological impression of shadow on one side of the face.
>
> DOWN LIGHTING - ideally each acting area should have it's own down light. This provides a 3-D effect to the head.
>
> BACK LIGHTING - ideally each acting area should also have it's own back light. This gives a halo effect, and defines the head and shoulders, making the performer "pop" out from the background.
>
> "SHIN BUSTERS" - mounted on free standing light trees on the sides of the stage deck. Usually for dance lighting. Defines the whole body.

LIGHTING THE SET

When lighting a set, take these elements into consideration.

> BACKDROPS – give these their own washes to avoid lines from stray instruments.
>
> CURTAINS - usually not lit other than from spill light from area lighting.
>
> CYCLORAMA OR "CYC" - solid flat back drop, can be flat along the back of the stage or encircle the stage, hence the name "cyclorama". Usually white. Lit from the front at a steep angle, from instruments from the pipe above, and/or from floor mounted instruments. A cyc is one of the most expensive items in a high school theatre. There are only a few places in the world that make them, and they are one seamless piece of material that can be as wide as 40' or more. Students should be taught not to touch a cyc. I tell students their cyc likely costs more than their parents' cars!

SCRIM – a see-through mesh back drop. Can be white, black or painted with a scene. Lit from the same direction as a cyc. If lit from the front appears as solid wall. If lit from the back, it's see through. Likewise, should be handled with extreme care.

SPECIALS - fireplaces, doorways, etc. Usually lit from hidden fixtures in or behind the set, gelled appropriate colors. Eg: a fireplace would be lit from one or more small instruments, gelled with reds and oranges, a doorway would be back lit from above, with the appropriate color gel, depending on whether the door led to another room or to the outside.

VARYING LEVELS - most sets will have different levels that the actors use. In general, each level should be treated as its own acting area and lit accordingly.

EFFECT AND MOOD LIGHTING

Actors should be enhanced with more than area lights. Ideally two or three color washes should be available, and each area should have a down and/or back light. Other effects are also useful.

FRONT WASH - this is generally from several instruments hung from the house that are aimed from straight on. By itself a wash is very "flat" and does not pick out the features of the face by the use of shadow. Best used in conjunction with area lighting for washing the stage with color, for example: for suggesting night time (dark blue). Ideally three color washes should be available in your rep plot.

HIGH SIDES - this can be used for molding or color effects. And can, for instance, suggest a sunrise.

GOBOS - Thin metal patterned templates that can be slipped into ellipsoidal instruments. These can pattern the stage, such as a dappled leaf effect on the floor, and actors as they move through the dappled light, or they can depict a specific object such as a moon on a back drop or perhaps light coming through a window.

COLOR

Color is used extensively in theatre lighting. Even a "white" light that you see probably has a color filter on it. In the theatre these color filters are called gels. Some are so subtle, that they even have names such as "No Color Blue".

Color is used to depict mood, location, time of day, and so on. Rudimentary examples include blue or lavender for nighttime, green for a forest, or amber for a sunset. Warm colors are usually associated with comedy and cool colors with tragedy. Color can also be used to enhance people's skin tones. Some notorious actresses are renown for demanding a certain gel color in the lights to enhance their skin tone.

The color our eyes see is the product of the color of light and the color of every object and person on the stage. Let's look at why this is.

WHITE LIGHT

"White" light is made up of many colors, usually considered to be seven or eight colors: red, orange, yellow, green, blue-green, blue, indigo, violet.

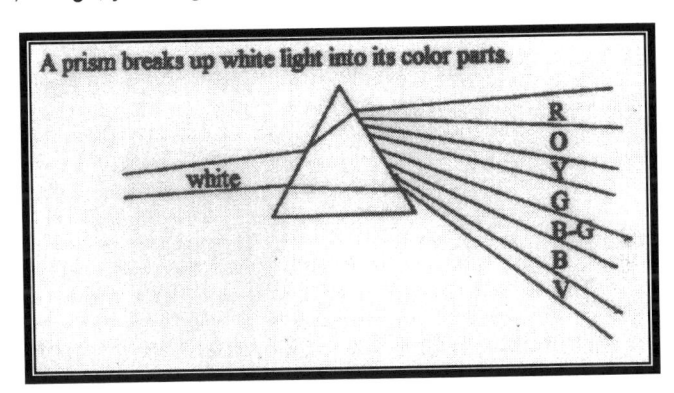

A prism breaks up white light into its color parts.

When you see "white" light it is rarely pure white; meaning, an exact mix of all of the colors. All white light has a "color temperature", based on the temperature of a "black burning body", which affects what color "white" it is. A "cooler" "bluer" light has a higher color temperature. A "warmer" "amber" light has a lower color temperature. Think about a fire pit. The hottest ambers in the middle that have been burning a long time are a very cold bluish white in color, while the (relatively) colder edges of the outer flames are very warm and amber in color.

COLORED LIGHT

Given colors can also have a variety of hidden colors. For example, there are a lot of pink gels that are very similar to look at, but some tend to the yellow and some tend to the blue. Take for instance Rosco® gels numbers 33 through 37.

R33	No Color Pink	A warm tan tint.
R34	Flesh Pink	Has a hidden orange, can look peachy.
R35	Light Pink	More yellow than R33, makes greens pop out.
R36	Medium Pink	Orangey, more saturated than R34.
R37	Pale Rose Pink	A more saturated blue-ish pink.

Similarly, a blue gel can tend to the red or to the green. A blue gel with a bit of red in it might be good for suggesting a warm summer night, while a blue gel with a bit of green tint to it might be good for a tragic or scary scene, or a cold winter night. A blue gel with a slight red tint to it will make skin tones more appealing than one with a green tint.

There is really no such thing as a pure color gel. Even green gels can have a bit of red in them. Try this with a Rosco 91 gel, called "Primary Green". Fold the gel into four and hold it up to an incandescent light source. What color do you see?

SATURATED LIGHT

You can think of saturation as how "deep" or "dark" a color is. A hot magenta pink gel is more saturated than a pastel baby pink gel. Gels transmit (let through) different amounts of light depending on their saturation. Gels with less pigment transmit more light than do gels that are saturated in pigment. Think back to your school chemistry class. A solution of water and salt is saturated once no more salt will dissolve into the water, making it look murky and hard to see through. A less saturated solution is easier to see through.

When lighting a night scene for example, use a dark blue. However, if you only used a dark blue it would be difficult for the audience to see your actors. So some other less saturated light would have to be added, probably from another direction. Saturated and less saturated gels can be used in combination to create effects, as the less saturated light will "cut through" the more saturated light.

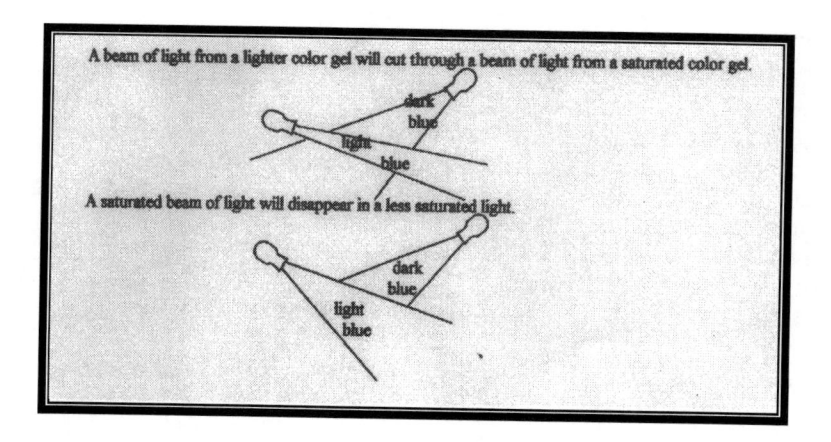

COLOR MIXING

Unlike paint, the primary colors of light are: RED GREEN BLUE

> Unlike paint, the primary colors of light are RED, BLUE, GREEN.
>
> The secondary colors of light:
> red + green = yellow
> red + blue = magenta
> green + blue = blue-green
>
> The secondary colors of paint:
> red + yellow = orange
> red + blue = violet
> yellow + blue = green
>
> LIGHT — Venn diagram with GREEN, BLUE, RED circles; overlaps show blue-green, yellow, magenta, and WHITE in the center.
>
> PAINT — Venn diagram with YELLOW, BLUE, RED circles; overlaps show green, orange, violet, and BLACK in the center.

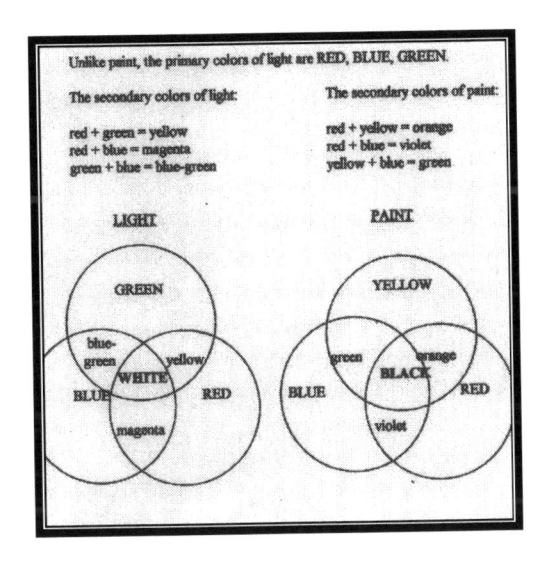

The colors of light can be combined, just as the colors of paint can be combined, to make countless colors. There are two ways to combine colors in light: additive mixing and subtractive mixing.

ADDITIVE COLOR MIXING

You use additive color mixing when colored lights coming from two or more instruments are combined. This is most noticed when lighting a cyc (the white drape at the back of a stage).

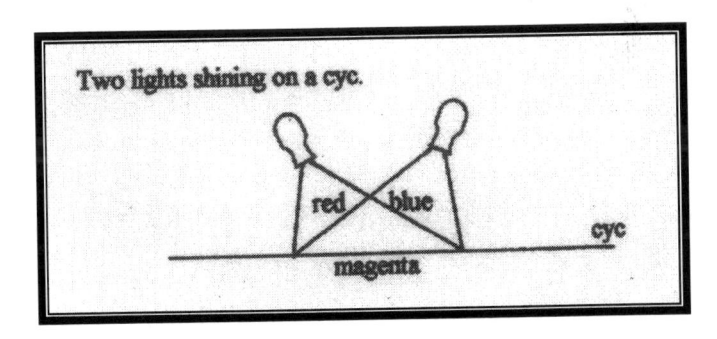

> Two lights shining on a cyc.
> red   blue
> magenta   cyc

Blue and red will make a magenta/purple/lavender color, while blue and green will make blue-green/teal. Red and green make – can you guess? – yellow. If beams of pure red, blue and green are mixed together the result will appear to be "white" light. Similarly, each primary color mixed with its opposite secondary color will also appear to be "white" light.

SUBTRACTIVE COLOR MIXING

Subtractive mixing is something you won't find in paint, only in light. You use subtractive mixing when two or more gels are placed in a single instrument.

For instance, suppose you place a yellow gel and a blue gel in a light. The color of the beam of light would be green.

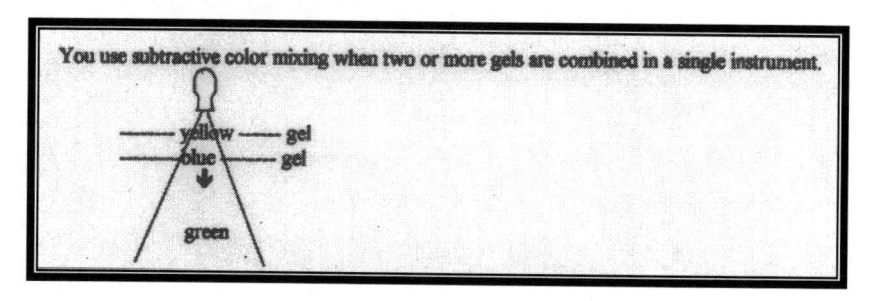

```
You use subtractive color mixing when two or more gels are combined in a single instrument.
        yellow ——— gel
        blue  ——— gel
           ↓
         green
```

Why is this?

First the full spectrum of light coming from the lamp in the instrument encounters the yellow gel. The yellow gel only lets through the yellow, red and green parts of the spectrum. The other colors of the spectrum are not transmitted, or in other words are "subtracted".

Next the yellow, red and green parts of the spectrum encounter the blue gel. This blue gel only lets through the blue, green and blue-green parts of the spectrum. However there are no blue parts of the spectrum hitting it as the blue was subtracted by the yellow gel. So therefore the only part of the available spectrum to get through is the green.

Another way of looking at this would be:

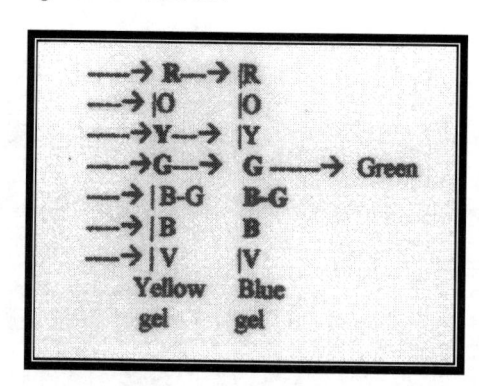

```
    ——→ R ——→  R
    ——→ |O      |O
    ——→ Y ——→  |Y
    ——→ G ——→  G ——→ Green
    ——→ |B-G   B-G
    ——→ |B     B
    ——→ |V     |V
        Yellow  Blue
        gel     gel
```

Similarly adding a pure orange gel with a pure violet gel will result in no light being transmitted.

22

The orange gel would only let through the red, orange and yellow parts of the spectrum. The violet gel will only let through the blue, violet and red parts of the spectrum, but none of those parts of the spectrum are hitting it, so it results in no light getting through.

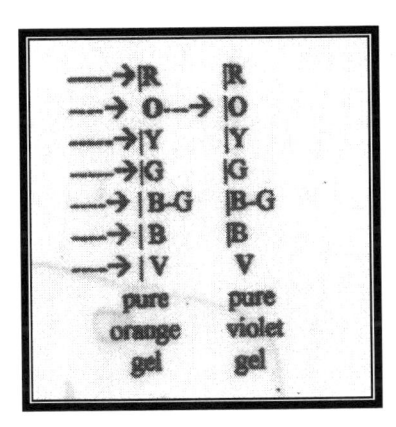

```
———→ R        R
———→ O ——→ O
———→ Y        Y
———→ G        G
———→ |B-G    B-G
———→ |B       B
———→ |V       V
     pure     pure
    orange   violet
      gel     gel
```

CHOOSING GELS

Most of a Lighting Designer's gel choices will be made by feelings and instinctive reaction to the color, not from scientific data, and not from the instrument readings that film lighting relies on. That said, it's still good to have a basic understanding of the scientific data. Light waves are measured in Angstroms. A violet or blue light wave has a shorter wave length than a red light wave.

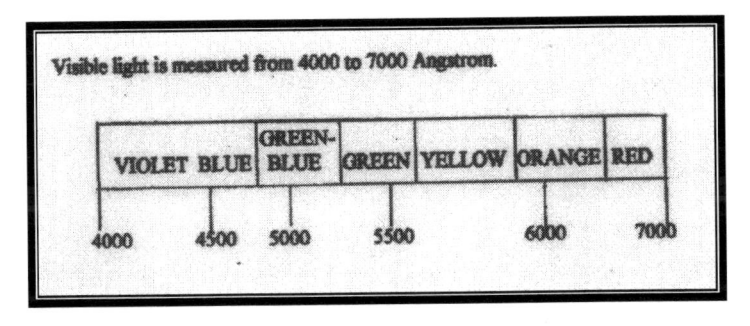

Visible light is measured from 4000 to 7000 Angstrom.

VIOLET	BLUE	GREEN-BLUE	GREEN	YELLOW	ORANGE	RED
4000	4500	5000	5500	6000		7000

Most gel brands have a white card behind each gel in a gel book (essentially a swatch book) with a graph of a color spectrum. This 'at-a-glance' graph lets lighting designers know what colors to expect in a gel. Sometimes just looking at a gel doesn't give the whole picture. The color of any actual gel may not completely reflect the color you get when it's put in front of a stage light. As you saw in the pink gel examples and the R91 example above.

> Each gel is rated with this scale. For instance a red gel would look like this (mostly from the red end of the spectrum):
>
> 4000 4500 5000 6000 7000

THE COLOR OF AN OBJECT

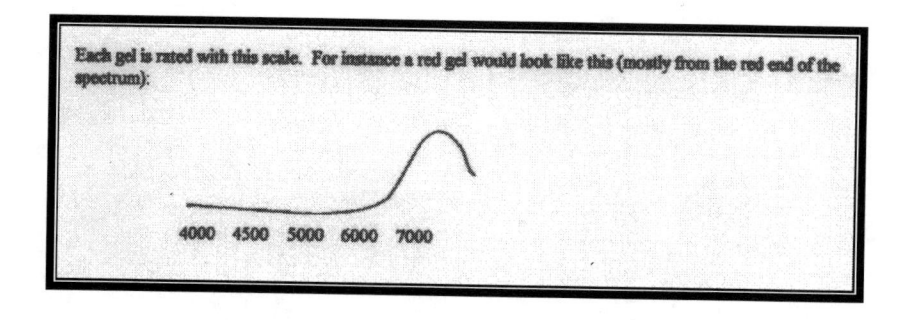

The color of an object can only be seen because its pigment acts as a reflector of light to the eye. For example, if the whole spectrum of light is being shone on a banana, the banana will only reflect the yellow light from the spectrum, so our eye perceives it as yellow. Similarly, if a blue object is lit with a blue or "white" light it will appear blue. If a pure blue object were lit with a pure red light it would make the object appear "black", because there is no blue light being applied to the object.

One application for this concept in the theatre would be a dancer in a purple costume, but where the lighting for the piece needs to be lit with an eerie green front wash. A purple costume with only green light shining on it would look a yucky brown. Bringing up a bit of lavender side-light would not ruin the green front wash lighting effect, but would bring out the purples in the costume. This a good example of color and distribution used in combination to create an effect.

MOVEMENT

Movement originally referred to "cuing", which is when the intensity of the light changes either up or down, or the other three properties change from one look to another. However, in the past three decades movement has also begun to refer to actual physical movement, because we now have lighting instruments that actually physically move.

But for our purposes here, the movement McCandless was referring to is each of the other three properties of light – intensity, distribution and color - being changed in some way. This is done when the light board operator executes a "cue", such as the lights fading up, fading down, crossfading or a complete blackout. This can be done slowly or very quickly (sometimes called a "bump").

MOTIVATED LIGHT

Unlike motivat<u>ing</u> light as a property of distribution, motivat<u>ed</u> light is a property of movement.

Most cues should be motivated. This means you should have a reason for every cue, whether in a play or a dance. Motivated light can move fast or slowly. A setting sun would call for a slowly executed cue. The ambient light from a table lamp on a set being switched on or off would call for a bump. In dance, the motivation might be the change in tempo of the music, or the entrance or exit of some dancers.

MCCANDLESS' LIGHT PLOT

So how do theatrical lighting designers apply this theoretical knowledge? Knowing this will help you to help them perform their job effectively.

In order to achieve optimal manipulation of these four properties McCandless developed a layout we call the Light Plot. A Light Plot can be designed from scratch for a specific show, or a Rep Plot (repertory plot) can be designed to accommodate multiple types of events. A Lighting Plot that is re-designed over and over again is more suited to the university level, where all the students are learning lighting as a vocational choice, and where it is necessary to start each lighting design "from scratch" for each show. In the high school theatre setting, there is usually very little time - or money - to completely re-design (and re-hang, re-focus, re-patch and re-cue) a Light Plot from scratch for each event, so a Rep Plot makes much more sense. A rep plot can be easily adapted to provide lighting for any event from class meetings, speeches, variety shows, band and choir concerts to plays, musicals and dance recitals.

AREA LIGHTING

A full rep plot is discussed later on, however the basis for a rep plot is the "Area" lighting, which evenly lights the stage. Following is a very basic diagram and explanation of the McCandless layout of area lighting.

AREA LIGHTING

Stanley McCandless developed a method of evenly lighting the acting area of the stage.

Divide the stage into roughly 8' circular acting areas. Number them from SL to SR, DS to US.

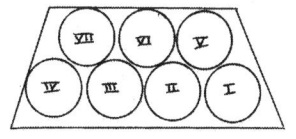

(VII) (VI) (V)
(IV) (III) (II) (I)

Ideally each area should have two front lights at a 45° angle vertically and in plan. (Not all pipe positions will allow for this precise angle.)

The lights from one side should be a warm colour (pink or amber) and the other a cool color (usually blue), this reproduces the natural effect of sunlight and shadow on the face.

McCandless started by dividing the stage into acting areas. Once the lighting designer has determined the amount of areas they need on a stage, they then must calculate the beam angle of light needed, which depends on the distance between the instrument and the area being lit. Once that is determined the appropriate instrument to do the job can be chosen. Each instrument has a rated beam angle that is determined by its reflector and lenses. We will address this more in depth later on as this knowledge not only helps the lighting designer, but also helps you know where to place your lighting positions so that the lighting designer working in your theatre doesn't come across the issues, such as shadowy faces, like Jo did in the opening vignette.

BEAM ANGLES AND FIELD ANGLES

Each instrument has both a "beam angle" and a "field angle". The beam angle is the 10% cut off of light and the field angle is the 50% cut off of light. When lighting a specific spot on the stage you would want to consider the beam angle of the light, because you need to know where the light ends. But in the case of area lighting you would want the field angle of the light, so that 50% of the light of one area overlaps with 50% of the light of another area, so that there is an even 100% spread of light across the stage.

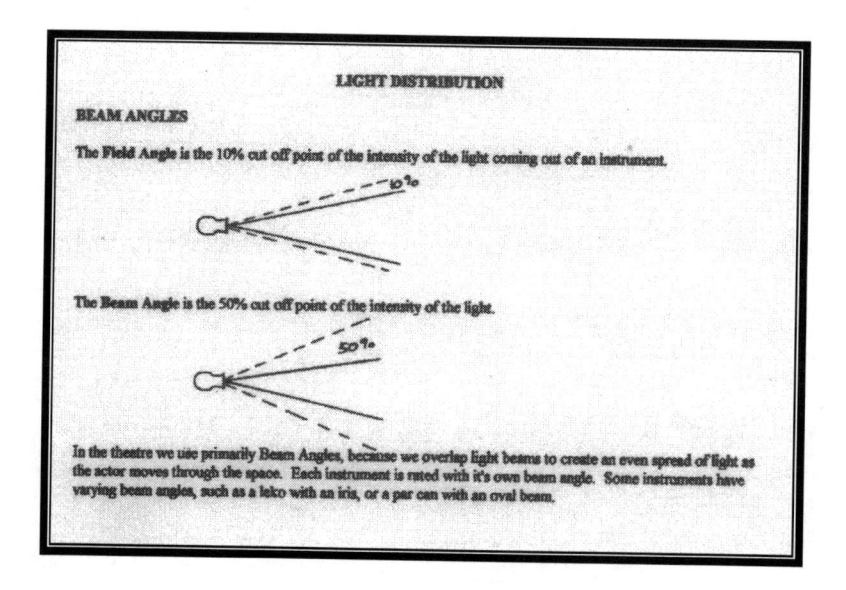

LIGHT DISTRIBUTION

BEAM ANGLES

The Field Angle is the 10% cut off point of the intensity of the light coming out of an instrument.

10%

The Beam Angle is the 50% cut off point of the intensity of the light.

50%

In the theatre we use primarily Beam Angles, because we overlap light beams to create an even spread of light as the actor moves through the space. Each instrument is rated with it's own beam angle. Some instruments have varying beam angles, such as a leko with an iris, or a par can with an oval beam.

CALCULATING BEAM ANGLES

Lets say a lighting designer has to accurately light a round wading pool in the middle of a stage with blue-green light from straight above (it's happened). In order to determine what instrument they need, a lighting designer would ask themselves, if I want an 6' diameter circular area to be lit from an instrument on a pipe that is 30' away, what beam angle instrument will I need. Conversely – lets say in the case of area lighting - before a lighting designer can ask that question in order to lay out their area lighting, architects would ask themselves if I want the lighting designer to be able to light an 8' circular area, which is 6' above the stage deck with a 19 degree instrument, with an overlap to the next area, how far away will I need to place the catwalk.

As an architect, you're probably no stranger to the math needed to calculate angles. To calculate what beam angle you need to light your wading pool you need to use trigonometry.

Let's say the electric above the wading pool is 22' off the stage deck. The radius is 3'. With the height at 22' and the length at 3' the way to find half the angle needed (we're using the radius, so we'd have to double it for the diameter), would be opposite over adjacent, which is the tangent of the angle. Double the result to find the whole angle, which would tell you what beam angle you would need to light the diameter of the pool.

If you're not into trig, another way would be to simply draw a scale diagram and simply measure.

27

CHAPTER 3

A LITTLE LIGHT PRACTICE

Let's leave the theatre for a moment and talk about light in general. In order for a theatrical lighting designer to design with light, they have to understand how light works. Probably as a part of your training you may have also had some theory about lighting, particularly if you are designing the lighting in buildings. The theory behind what light actually does is the same for a building as it is for a stage. If you've worked with lighting before, you probably have a good sense of why light is important, but let's have a general refresher.

WHY IS LIGHT IMPORTANT?

Light is important because it is crucial to human performance. Light affects the eye and the brain in so many ways. The human eye is enormously sensitive and adjustable. The manipulation of light in our environment can:

- increase productivity – better light (intensity, angle, no glare, etc) equals happier workers, equals harder work,
- affect health – for example, some people get SAD (Season Affective Disorder, a type of depression) and are helped by lights,
- be important for safety – bright light is needed for hazardous and detailed work,
- save energy – in one study office workers were given their own lighting controls at their desk, and they used less light, thus using less energy,
- influence mood and atmosphere – in another study a large group of people were placed in a bright room. They gathered in large groups and the volume of the conversation increased. When the same large group of people were placed in a room with dimmed lighting, they tended to gather small groups and the conversation level was much quieter.

Designers who work with light have to know a bit of:
    Physics
    Biology
    Math
    Psychology

There are many occupations where knowledge of the science of light is important, such as (in no particular order):

> ARCHITECTURE/LANDSCAPING (how light affects form and function),
> MEDICINE/BIOTECHNOLOGY (how light affects the body and health),
> EDUCATION (how light affects learning),
> ART/PHOTOGRAPHY (how light affects form),
> PERFORMING ARTS (how to light a stage),
> ENGINEERING (how to light a structure, roadway, etc.),
> GEOGRAPHY/METEOROLOGY/ENVIRONMENTAL SCIENCE (how light affects the earth),
> ASTRONOMY (how light is used in star analysis),
> PHYSICS (how light does what it does, why, and how to harness it for practical use),
> BOTANYZOOLOGY/BIOLOGY (how light affects plants, animals and living organisms),
> TELEVISION/FILM (how to light for the camera),
> URBAN DEVELOPMENT (light placement and avoidance of light pollution),
> AREOSPACE/AVAIATION (exterior and interior lighting in planes and spacecraft),
> HISTORY/SOCIOLOGY/ARCHEOLOGY/ANTHROPOLOGY (how light has affected our daily lives, from fires to LEDs),
> PSYCHOLOGY (the psychology of light and color and how it affects people).

In order to utilize the basics of the science of light, designers have to understand:

> how light reflects and refracts,
> how different wave lengths make different colors of light,
> how the eye perceives light and
> how people respond to light.

This is particularly true for stage lighting. Stage lighting has to mimic the real world or it wouldn't be acceptable to an audience. In stage lighting light is used to depict mood, location, time of day, it can be used to draw the audience's attention, to light a set, to light actors or dancers. And it has to do these things on a stage the same way it does in the real world for the human eye to accept it. Sometimes in a production without a set or specific dialogue, lighting can be the only indicator of these concepts, but the lighting still has to make sense.

It is important for a theatrical lighting designer to not only understand these concepts at a cerebral level, but to have experienced these concepts. It's also important for an architect designing a stage lighting system to have experienced what the theatrical lighting designer experiences, in order to make the choices that will allow the designer to do their job. This is particularly important in the educational setting, where these concepts are in turn being taught to students.

ACTIVITIES

In order to get a more visceral experience of what light does, following are six activities you can conduct yourself. While these may seem like something you did in school yourself, they're worth a refresher.

The activities are:

1. Bouncing and Bending
2. Relativity
3. Adaptation
4. What Color is Light?
5. Primary Colors
6. What Color is That Tree?

You can do Activities 1,2 and 3 in any order, but Activities 4, 5 and 6 are best done in order as the knowledge scaffolds upon the previous activity.

PLEASE NOTE: For the activities that involve turning out the lights, it is best to be in a room where you can make it as dark as possible. The darker the room the more successful the activities will be.

All of the items used in these activities are common household items, so you can conduct these activities at home or in the office.

You will need:

> A stopwatch
> 3 large flashlights
> 1 small flashlight
> A mirror
> Clear glass or plastic
> A piece of flat foil
> A piece of crumpled foil
> A piece of wax paper
> A book
> A clear plastic cup (you will need to fill this with water)
> A tub (you will need to fill this with water)
> A piece of green cellophane
> A piece of red cellophane
> A piece of blue cellophane
> 3 rubber bands
> A piece of paper with red, green and blue color splashes

Most of these activities have "right/wrong" results, because this is the scientific-mathematical part of the art. At the end of the activities is a *Results and Reasons* section, which lists the results you should expect for each activity, plus some interesting facts. Let us begin...

ACTIVITY 1
BOUNCING AND BENDING

You will need:
> 1 large flashlight
> Objects to test:
>> A mirror
>> Clear glass or plastic
>> A piece of flat foil
>> A piece of crumpled foil
>> A piece of wax paper
>> A book
>> A clear plastic cup at least half full of water
>> Any other objects you'd like to test

Light travels in a straight line until it meets an object. When it encounters the object it does one of a number of things. It bounces off, bends in another direction, goes through the object, or is absorbed into the object.

- If the beam light is bounced back off the surface, this is called **Reflection**.

- If the light bends as a result of contact with the surface, this is called **Refraction**.

- If the light beam goes through the object and comes out the other side, this is called **Transmission**.

- If the light does not go through the object or bounce back off, this is called **Absorption**.

1. List the objects to test above on a sheet of paper.

2. Below each object state how you think the object with transform the light beam, using the vocabulary above. Hint: some objects will affect the beam of light in more than one way.

3. Once you have written your hypothesis turn out the lights and shine the flashlight at each object. Below your hypothesis record what actually happened.

4. Consider what properties of the materials altered the beam of light in what ways. Why do you think this is?

ACTIVITY 2
RELATIVITY

You will need:
1 small flashlight

1. Stand about 8 feet from a wall.

2. With the room lights on, shine the small flashlight at the wall.

3. How well can you see the beam of light from the flashlight on the wall?

4. Now turn out the lights and shine the flashlight at the wall.

5. Now how well can you see the beam of light from the flashlight on the wall?

6. Why do you think you got the results you did? Did the Intensity of the beam of light change?

7. Answer this age-old question: Are the stars shining during the day?

ACTIVITY 3
ADAPTATION

You will need:
    1 small flashlight
    A stopwatch

The brightness level of light is called ***Intensity***.

One way to measure the intensity of light is in *Footcandles*. There are probably about 30 footcandles on the surfaces in the room you are in right now, and you can probably see just fine.

Can you see ok at the beach on a sunny day? That's about 20,000 footcandles!

Have you ever walked outside at night with only the moonlight? That's about a ½ footcandle.

The eye is very good at adapting to a variety of intensities. The eye can see pretty well in dim lights and in bright light, but it can take a while to adapt. Let's see how long it takes your eyes to adapt.

1. Stand in a lit room. Make the room as bright as you can, turn on all the lights.

2. Look around at all the objects you can see. Note at least three very small objects that are across the room from you.

3. Now turn the lights out. Start your stop watch (you don't have to see it going.)

4. Look around and wait.

5. When you can see the three small objects you chose, stop your stopwatch and turn on the light.

6. Record how long it took until you could see the three objects.

7. Think about this: when you turned the lights back on did you have a reaction to the intensity of the light and if so, what? About how long did it take you to adjust to the sudden increase in intensity?

ACTIVITY 4
WHAT COLOR IS LIGHT?

You will need:
    A mirror
    A tub of water
    A large flashlight

Look around you. What color is the light?

You can make your own prism and find out what color light is.

1. Fill the tub about two thirds full of water.

2. Place the tub on a table or on the floor a few feet away from a wall.

3. Hold the mirror in the water at the end of the tub furthest from the wall (the water should come about half way up the mirror), so that the mirror is facing the wall. Lean the mirror in the water at an angle.

4. Hold the flashlight at the other end of the box, opposite the mirror. The flashlight shines away from the wall.

5. Turn on the flashlight. Shine the flashlight on the part of the mirror that is in the water.

6. Look at the reflection on the wall.

7. What colors do you see in the reflection of the light on the wall? What color is it around the edges in particular? Where did the colors come from if the flashlight is white light and the water is clear?

ACTIVITY 5
PRIMARY COLORS

You will need:
>3 flashlights (all the same)
>A piece of green cellophane
>A piece of red cellophane
>A piece of blue cellophane
>3 rubber bands

What are the primary colors of paint? What are the primary colors of light? Paint (or pigment) has different primary colors than light. The primary colors of light are *red*, *blue* and *green*.

If you add the primary colors of light together what color will you get? Try it:

1. Cover each flashlight with each piece of cellophane (you may need to use two or more layers) and secure with a rubber band.

2. Turn on the three flashlights. You should have one red light, one blue light and one green light.

3. Shine all the flashlights onto the same spot on the wall from the same distance. Make sure you have a white wall. If not, you can pin up a piece of white paper.

4. Record what color the combination of the light is. Give your reasons why you think this is. Compare this activity to the activity you did with the prism. What's going on?

ACTIVITY 6
WHAT COLOR IS THAT TREE?

You will need:
3 flashlights (all the same)
    A piece of green cellophane
    A piece of red cellophane
    A piece of blue cellophane
    3 rubber bands
    Color splash paper

We've learned how light can be different colors, but what about objects? All matter has a chemical in it called *Pigment*. Different pigments either absorb or reflect part or parts of white light. When we say an apple is red, this is because the pigments absorb all the colors in the light expect red, which is reflected.

A beam of light or a *light source* can be a color, or you can put a filter over a "white" light source, therefore making the light source that color. If you have a filter, say red, this color passes through, but the other colors are absorbed by the filter.

This activity will help you answer these two questions:
1. Most plants are green. What color light do the chemicals in plants primarily need to help the plant live?
2. Why do things look bluer in fluorescent lights, and yellower in parking lot lights?

    1. Cover each flashlight with each piece of cellophane (you may need to use two or more layers) and secure with a rubber band. You should have one red light, one blue light and one green light.

    2. Turn out the lights.

    3. Shine the red light onto the color splash paper.

    4. What colors do you see on the color splash paper?

    5. Shine the blue light onto the color splash paper.

    6. What colors do you see on the color splash paper?

    7. Shine the green light onto the color splash paper.

    8. What colors do you see on the color splash paper?

    9. Which color splashes turned black under which color light? Which color splashes stayed the same color? What happened to the white paper around the color splashes; what color did that change to each time? What do you think is happening? Why do some of the color splashes appear to turn black and some stay the same color.

Now answer the two original questions above.

RESULTS AND REASONS

This section lists the expected results of each activity.

1. BOUNCING AND BENDING

A mirror	Reflection
Clear glass or plastic	Transmission
A piece of flat foil	Reflection
A piece of crumpled foil	Reflection and Refraction
A piece of wax paper	Refraction and Transmission
A book	Absorption
A clear plastic cup with water	Refraction and Transmission

A theatrical lighting designer has to consider the materials of sets and costumes in their design choices, and how they will affect the lighting.

2. RELATIVITY
You should not be able to see the beam of light on the wall with the room lights on. Once the room lights are off the beam of light should be visible on the wall.
Light is relative. If there is a brighter light, then another light might appear less bright, until it is the brightest light. For instance, do the stars shine during the day? Yes, they do, but we just can't see them. Our sun/star is closer to us and therefore relatively brighter. When we turn the sun out (ie: nighttime) we can see the stars.

In the theatre a brighter light can "cut" through a dimmer light, the same goes for color saturation – a less saturated light will cut through a more saturated light because the more saturated a gel is the less amount of light it lets through.

3. ADAPTATION
The eye takes only about a minute to adapt to a brighter light, but it can take up to an hour to adapt to dimmer light.

One way light adaption can play out in the theatre is in cuing. Light cue #1 can look just fine to the audience. Then light cue #2 comes along which is brighter, so the audience's eyes adapt. Then for cue #3 we go back to the same as cue #1. The audience will perceive cue #3 as darker than cue #1, even though they are the same, because their eyes adapted to the higher intensity of cue #2.

The same happens with color. Let's say we're at a dance concert. Dance #1 has amber lighting, then dance #2 has bright pink lighting. Dance #3 again calls for the same amber lighting as #1, but it looks dingy. That's because the eye adapted to another color and started to "color correct". Which brings us to...

4. WHAT COLOR IS LIGHT?
Where did all those colors come from? Light is in fact made up of many colors. They are in the light. We split up the colors in white light using a prism, which changes the direction or angle of the different wavelengths of the light that passes through it and splits them apart.

Imagine light as waves in the ocean. Some are long waves, some are short. Imagine a picket fence on the beach. As the waves hit that picket fence, some go through, but the long waves are going to go through at a different angle than the short waves and so will split into different directions on the other side of the fence. Red has the longest wave length and bends the least, and blue has the shortest wave length and bends the most. Light wave lengths are measured in nanometers, One nanometer equals ten angstroms. One angstrom equals one hundred-millionth of a centimeter. One angstrom is the diameter of a hydrogen atom, the smallest element. In other words a light wavelength is very, very small.

In the theatre we can change the color of light coming out of an instrument by putting a gel in front of it. Each gel lets through specific parts of the spectrum.

5. PRIMARY COLORS

You should see white light (or *whitish* light depending on the purity of the cellophane colors). This is called Additive Color Mixing. The prism split up the white light into it's various colors. Adding the three primary colors combines the light to make white again. These two activities are opposites.

In the theatre, mixing primary colors is predominately used in cyc lighting, because with just the three primary colors of light an awful lot of color choices can be made.

6. WHAT COLOR IS THAT TREE?

The color of an object depends upon the color of the light source. For instance, under the red filter, blue and green objects appear black. This is because there is no blue or green in the red light source. The pigment of the blue ink only reflects blue, but as there is no blue in the light source the ink appears black. The pigment of the green ink only reflects green, but as there is no green in the light source the ink appears black. The white paper reflects all colors, but as there is only red in the light source, the white paper can only reflect the red (it can't reflect a color that isn't shining on it).

As for the green plant (assuming plants are all green) the pigment that does the absorbing is called chlorophyll. Chlorophyll absorbs red and blue light for the plant to use. The remaining light is mostly green and therefore gives plants (or at least, leaves) their greenish color.

The fluorescent light source doesn't have many reds or yellows in it, so the light can appear bluish. Remember, the color pigment of the object can't be reflected if the color isn't in the light source to begin with. Parking lot lights don't have many blues in their source, so most cars in a car park with yellowish lights look some shade of orangey-brown.

In the theatre the lighting designer must work closely with the set designer and costume designer to chose color palettes that will enhance the colors of the sets and costumes, not change the colors that the set and costume designers have originally chosen, which is a problem Jo encountered in the opening vignette.

CHAPTER 4

EQUIPMENT

Now that you have an understanding of what light does, we will look at the instruments that house, and manipulate, the light sources. What instruments, and how many of each kind, do you need to spec? Before you can determine this, you need to know what each type is commonly used for. This also links into the lighting positions and the number of circuits needed.

INSTRUMENTS

There are many types of instruments that are used in stage lighting. We will look at the most popular types used in high schools. They are:

ELLISPOIDAL/LEKO/"SOURCE FOUR"

The terms "ellipsoidal", "leko" and "source four" are used interchangeably. The term "leko" was more commonly used in the 80's and comes from a brand of lights called "Leko Lights". "Source Four" is actually a brand name, but these days it has become common for some people use it to describe this specific instrument, even though there are Source Four PARs, Source Four fresnels, etc. You can tell a lighting technician's age by which term they use!

For our purposes, here we will use the term "ellipsoidal". An ellipsoidal has, as its name suggests, an ellipsoidal shaped reflector with two focal points (yes – tech theatre does use math), plus two plano-convex lenses (flat on one side, rounded on the other side), along with a sliding barrel that allows the light beam to be focused with a hard edge (technically called a 'hard focus') and a soft/diffuse edge (technically called 'fuzzy-wuzzy' – ok, technically called a 'soft focus'). Because this instrument can be focused it can also house a metal or glass pattern that can be projected onto the stage. By substituting different barrels, which have their lenses positioned differently, you can also change the beam angle. The most common beam angles ellipsoidals come in is 19, 26, 36 and 50 degrees. There are wider and narrower available too. Ellipsoidals also come in "Zooms" which can change the beam angle from around 25 degrees to 50 degrees. These are great for versatility. They are great as spare instruments as it takes the guess work out of how many of what angle to keep on hand.

Ellipsoidals also have built in shutters that allow you to further control the light – for instance, if you just wanted to light a doorway you could shutter off all four sides so that no light spilled on the surrounding walls. Ellipsoidals are usually used for area lighting, and specials. They can also be used for washes, especially if you want to put in a break up pattern gobo (often in the case of dance).

FRESNEL

Loosely pronounced "fre-nel". You may have heard this term in connection with lighthouses. This instrument has the same fresnel lens that lighthouses do. This lens is 'stepped' and can therefore create an almost parallel beam of light – as used in lighthouses, and also in those annoying traffic lights that you can only see once you pull into that lane. In theatre though, the lens is usually formed to create a nice evenly flooded spread of light. By moving the reflector and lamp closer or further away from the lens you can "flood" or "spot" the beam angle. Unlike the ellipsoidal where you have to replace the barrel in order to change the beam angle, the fresnel has the capability to change the beam angle within the instrument. However, you give up the hard focus that the ellipsoidal allows, as fresnels only have a soft focus. Fresnels are mostly used for, downs, backs, general washes and specials.

PAR

P.A.R. stands for 'parabolic aluminized reflector'. A PAR has a reflector that is usually made of aluminum and is in the shape of a parabola. A PAR gives a fairly parallel beam, which can be adjusted by the use of different lenses. Also, depending on the lens patterns, the light beam of a PAR can be oval, not circular. This allows you to better control where the light goes, from an instrument that isn't focusable. PARs are usually used as washes, sides and specials. They are often used as ladder lighting for dance. There is also an instrument called a Par-nel, which is a combination of the fresnel and the PAR.

MULTI-PARS

As the name suggests, multi-pars are a multiple amount of PARs combined in one instrument. The most common configuration is three, to allow for RGB (red-green-blue) color mixing. Multi-pars can be used for down lighting or even side lighting. They can also be used for cyc lighting for smaller cycs. Multi-pars usually have dedicated colored lenses, instead of needing gels.

CYC

Cyc lights come in many different types and configurations, but their main purpose is to light the cyc. They are typically hung in configurations of three, again to allow for RGB color mixing.

FIXTURES VS INSTRUMENTS

One term that is incorrectly used in the theatre by non-theatre folks is "fixtures" when intending to refer to "instruments". The term fixtures is commonly used in architectural lighting, whether you are an architect or a homeowner. In the theatre we use the term instruments. Fixtures are *fixed* or installed and usually cannot be moved. Instruments on the other hand can be hung, focused, taken down, moved and hung again. In a theatre the work lights and house lights can be considered fixtures, while the production lights are considered instruments.

A LAMP, BY ANY OTHER NAME

But, there is an even bigger faux pas in the theatrical lighting world. And that is: calling a lamp a "light bulb". The correct term – also in the architectural lighting world – is "lamp". The "bulb" is just the glass part. A "lamp" consists of the bulb, the gas, the element and the base.

SPEC'ING THE LIGHTING PACKAGE

Following is a sample lighting package for a stage using McCandless, with:
  20 acting areas (4 zones deep with 5 areas across)
  3 ladders
  The cyc on the 3rd electric
  No catwalk directly above the apron

SAMPLE LIGHTING INSTRUMENT PACKAGE
FOR BASIC HIGH SCHOOL REP PLOT

#	Type	Purpose	Location
10	19 deg Ellipsoidal	Zone 1 Areas	2nd Beam
10	26 deg Ellipsoidal	Zone 2 Areas	2nd Beam
10	26 deg Ellipsoidal	Zone 3 Areas	1st Beam
10	36 deg Ellipsoidal	Zone 4 Areas	1st Electric
20	Fresnel	Cool Downs	1st, 2nd, 3rd Electrics
20	Fresnel	Warm Downs	1st, 2nd, 3rd Electrics
12	50 deg Ellipsoidal	3 Color Washes	2nd Beam
2	50 deg Ellipsoial	Break-up Gobos	SL and SR Galleries
4	36 deg Ellipsoidal	Cyc Gobos	1st Electric
24	PAR	Ladder lighitng	Galleries & Ladders
5	3-cell Cyc Lights	Cyc	3rd Electric
1	19 deg Ellipsoidal	Conductor Light	SL Gallery
2	26 deg Ellipsoidal	Choir Fill Light	SL and SR Galleies
8 to 12	Zoom Ellipsoidal	Spares	Storage
6	Fresnel	Spares	Storage
6	PAR	Spares	Storage

Again, by designing the lighting package backwards – assessing the size of the stage, deciding on the lighting method, deciding where the lighting positions need to be, then deciding what instruments are needed to achieve this - we can avoid the problems that Jo the lighting designer had in the opening vignette with not having the right amount of instruments and the right types to do her job.

WHICH LIGHT BOARD?

As well as spec'ing a lighting instrument package, if you are designing a theatre, you will be faced with the decision of what light board to choose in order to control all of the instruments. You don't want to be in a situation such as the opening vignette where Jo found that the light board is too high tech to be of any practical use in a high school theatre. If you don't foresee your high school purchasing $2000.00 moving lights for their theatre, and having a professional career training program for a student lighting crew who will be learning light board programming for moving lights, then there is no need to have a light board sophisticated enough to control moving lights. Leave that for when the vocational student gets to university or starts an apprenticeship. The same may go for LED lights. LED lights are becoming more common, however they require programming that goes beyond most high school staff's ability. The best thing to do is to confer with the people who will actually be using the equipment about their knowledge level, their educational plans for their theatre, and their operations budget, before spec'ing anything considered 'state-of-the-art' in a high school theatre.

Another thing to avoid is a small light board that has a multitude of functions. While a smaller less expensive light board with a lot of functions sounds like a good idea on the surface, some of these compact boards have so many functions that they've had to get very creative in how to access each function. There are so many steps, with functions hidden within functions that it makes it too difficult for students, who come and go, to learn and retain how the board works. Be careful that the light board that you spec or purchase doesn't have too many steps/modes to go through just to perform simple functions such as patching, recording, play back, etc.

Some light boards these days don't have faders for channels and rely only on key pad entry. The choice of whether to go with one of these boards depends on the uses of your theatre and who the users will be. I personally find key pad entry too slow. When I'm designing lights I talk pretty fast and I want my light board operator to keep up. I have to grit my teeth when I say "Bring channel 46 to 80 percent" and I have to wait to hear tap (Channel), tap (4), tap (6), tap (@), tap (8), tap (0), tap (Enter/*), when the light board op could have just reached over and in one movement and moved a fader to 80. Of course, these days kids are so used to completing tasks electronically instead of physically, and there can be reasons why you would want a key pad entry in a more sophisticated situation. Again, it boils down to planning ahead and questioning the people who will be using the equipment who are their users and what are the uses of the board. At least with a board with faders the operator has the option to use faders or the key pad, but with a board with only a key pad the operator does not have that option.

In addition, also watch out for light boards that don't use standard industry nomenclature, such as "Cues" and "Subs", for instance. With these boards students don't learn the common terms that are used in the rest of the live theatre industry, and those who already know the common terms will have to re-learn a set of new terms.

To reiterate (in case I haven't said it enough...), state-of-the-art is not always the best choice for a high school theatre. When deciding on a light board remember to ask these questions:

- Will the theatre be primarily used by students who come and go every few years?
- Will there be vocational training for students?
- How many students a year will want to learn to be lighting technicians?
- Will the theatre be staffed by professional technicians?
- Will the technicians run the theatre, and/or work with the students?
- Will the theatre be rented to outside users?
- Who will staff outside events, professional staff or students?
- Will outside users expected to be able to run their own lights?
- Will outside users be permitted to use the theatre's equipment unsupervised?
- Who will restore the equipment each time in preparation for the next user?

There is a school of thought that high school students should have the best technology available because they will soon go to a college or get a job where this technology is used and they will have a head start. However, in a high school setting, usually the need to have an easy to learn and operate light board trumps the need to have the best technology (*unless* there is a professional vocational training program at the high school).

This is primarily because most high school theatre departments have students who come and go. If you're lucky you will have a freshman come in with a keen interest in lighting and stay for four years. But what usually happens is either, that students come in expressing an interest and soon discover it's not for them, or a student who is vocationally passionate has always thought the Drama program was only for actors, and only discovers tech in his/her junior or senior year.

In addition, most typical Drama teachers really don't know much tech. They take one look at the light board and leave it up to a student to figure out, which results in the situation that Jo encountered in the opening vignette. Regardless of what light board you have it's best to hire professional technicians who will be there to mentor the students, which allows the Drama teacher to get on and do what they do best which is teaching acting, and directing students.

LIGHT BOARD PLACEMENT

Unlike a sound board which must be in the house so that the sound board operator can hear what the audience hears in real time and is constantly having to adjust the sound levels and quality during a production, a light board can be in the booth, because typically the light board operator has all the cues pre-programmed and only needs to push the Go button when the Stage Manager says "Go". During the design process the Lighting Designer will sit in the house so that she can see what the audience sees when she is choosing light levels and setting cues, and she will relay the light levels and cue timing over a headset to the light board operator who records them on the board in the booth.

During smaller events where the light board operator acts as the Lighting Designer, her line of vision is not interrupted from the booth to the stage, like a sound board operator's hearing would be affected if the sound board were in the booth, so she can design from the board. This isn't the ideal situation because the light board operator isn't seeing exactly what the audience sees, so whenever possible a Lighting Designer and light board operator should work in tandem.

Worse is a booth where the windows don't open. A lighting designer having to design from the booth above the audience's heads is bad enough, but having to look through glary glass makes it particularly difficult to design. Be sure that your booth has sliding glass windows.

The other solution is to bring the light board into the house. Your theatre should have a second location where the light board can be plugged in at the center of the house. This is so that a light board operator can simultaneously design and operate the lights while seeing what the audience sees. It's also convenient and less time consuming even when there is both a Lighting Designer and a light board operator, so that the Lighting Designer can just glance at the light board when she needs some information and then can directly give the light board operator her instructions without having to ask questions first.

CHAPTER 5

LEDS AND MOVING LIGHTS

So far we have only looked at traditional incandescent instruments. Most high school theatres don't have many, if any, LEDs or moving lights, so for our purposes here we won't go into them much other than to say that DMX capability is standard in new high school theatres these days and is probably here to stay. The trouble is that most high school theatres can't afford LEDs or moving lights. In addition, they can't afford educators who can teach the students on the correct operations. So even if high schools do have LEDs or moving lights provided for them in their lighting package, they often go unused, which is money that could have been spent on more traditional lighting fixtures. Remember the mega overkill, ultra expensive state-of-the-art light board installed with a complete system of programmable LED lights in the 100-seat school theatre? The theatre wasn't used for the first year and a half, and there are still three LED ellipsoidals sitting in the booth unused.

Again it's a case of designing backwards with the school administrators. State-of-the-art is not always the best choice for a high school theatre. When deciding on whether to spec LEDs or moving lights ask the administration these questions:

- Will the theatre be primarily used by students who come and go every few years?
- Will there be vocational training for students?
- How many students a year will want to learn to be lighting technicians?
- Will the theatre be staffed by professional technicians?
- Will the technicians run the theatre, and/or work with the students?
- Will the theatre be rented to outside users?
- Who will staff outside events, professional staff or students?
- Will outside users be allowed to use the theatre equipment unsupervised?
- Who will restore the equipment each time in preparation for the next user?

LED CYC LIGHTS

That all said, LED cyc lights in particular can add a boost to your lighting system. You can attain jewel like colors on your cyc that make your whole design pop. If you are going to install LED cyc lights be aware of the amount of channels they will take up, and how time consuming it is to control these independently. You will want to patch groups of lights to channels or subs.

There are also wireless communication controls for LED lights that make it a lot easier to move them around, which is particularly useful if your move your cyc several times a year. They're a bit pricey, but they will save the school money in the long run in terms of labor.

GPAC CYC CHEAT SHEET

SR ADDRESS	361	306	311		316	321	326		331	336	341		346	351	356	SL
R	301	302	303	R	304	305	306	R	307	308	309	R	310	311	312	R
G	321	322	323	G	324	325	326	G	327	328	329	G	330	331	332	G
B	341	342	343	B	344	345	346	B	347	348	349	B	350	351	352	B
A	361	362	363	A	364	365	366	A	367	368	369	A	370	371	372	A
M	381	382	383	M	384	385	386	M	387	388	389	M	390	391	392	M

MOVING LIGHTS

Moving lights are prohibitively expensive for a high school theatre budget, plus in order to operate them the operator has to know the programming. There are some inexpensive and easy to operate mirrored moving lights, gobo rotators and gel scrollers that mimic the automation of true programmable moving lights. These are not usually spec'd in the initial lighting package and are purchased later by the school, but it's good to make the administration aware of some options for the students to experience.

CHAPTER 6

A SYSTEM FOR ALL

When I first came on board at one theatre, one performing arts teacher complained to me that another performing arts teacher was always leaving the lighting system set up one way, and that teacher complained to me that the other teacher was always leaving the lighting system set up another way. The third performing arts teacher stayed out of the fray because she didn't know how to operate the lighting system at all and would rely on the others to set it up and run it for her. The few outside events that came into the theatre at that time were frustrated by the amount of time it took them to figure out how to use the lighting system while they were paying for the rental on an hourly rate.

REP PLOT

Although every event that comes into a theatre is unique, there is a way to provide a lighting system that can easily be applied to many uses of the space with only small adjustments that need to be made for specific requirements of a show or event. This is called a Rep Plot (short for Repertory Plot).

A Rep Plot is a standardized lighting system, which is versatile for almost all performances, from plays and musicals, to concerts and ballets, to speakers and videos, and allows for show-specific flexibility within a reasonable time frame. If your budget allows, be sure your rep plot is as extensive as possible, if not, choose as best you can from this list:

The Rand Rep Plot Model

Area lights – for 8' acting areas
One back light per area
One top light per area
Down washes – 3 colors
Front washes – 3 colors
Side washes – 3 colors
Break-up gobo patterns – from side and/or front
A center special
Cyc lights
Cyc grazing gobos
Cyc gobos – 3 across

Another reason it's very important to have an understanding of a rep plot is so that you know what instruments to provide in your specs. One high school that hired me to design their rep plot in their Black Box theatre had been provided a lighting packet from a local lighting supplier that had no forethought as to the functions that the lights would be needed for. For instance, the school was supplied with 18 26-degree ellipsoidals. Presumably the designer was thinking that these could be used for the area lights. That would be true in a main stage theatre, but the pipes in a Black Box theatre are comparatively low, so a 26-degree instrument has too narrow a beam spread. It would have been better if they'd provided a combination of 36 and 50-degree instruments. As it was, we had to limit the function of the theatre because there were not enough instruments of the correct beam spread to do anything more than create a proscenium stage in the space.

If you are in on the planning stages of a high school theatre, be sure not to lay out where circuits go and then spec the lighting instrument package. Instead, design backwards, and lay out a rep plot and then decide where the circuits need to go based on your rep plot, in order to achieve an optimal lighting system, and then spec the type and number of instruments needed to achieve that. I can't count the number of high school theatres I've been in which don't have enough circuits in the correct positions, or which don't have the right number of the right type of instruments, in order to achieve the versatile rep plot required for the variety of events that use a high school theatre.

CHEAT SHEET

In order to keep all of this information straight, Lighting Designers create a document that gives all users an at-a-glance overview of the Rep Plot for quick reference and easy use. This is frequently called the Cheat Sheet or Magic Sheet.

Following is an example of a Cheat Sheet. Note that all of the standard positions are set, and that an area is available in which to record specials. Specials customize a Rep Plot into a unique design for each event.

The Areas are laid out and numbered on the cheat sheet the same as they are on the stage. For instance, Area 1 is downstage right on the stage, so Area 1 is at the bottom left hand corner of the box. Remember that stage right is on your left as you look at the stage. The cheat sheet should always be laid out from the designer's perspective.

A note: it is traditional to number your areas from stage left to stage right – so as the designer you would see 5 4 3 2 1 – however I much prefer to have my areas run 1 2 3 4 5, the way I would read them, so I number them that way. It's a personal preference, so neither is wrong. But, it's important to find out from the user which way they prefer.

The downs box and the washes box are also laid out as the instruments are actually laid out, so that the designer has a quick reference.

SAMPLE REP PLOT CHEAT SHEET

AREAS

16	17	18	19	20
11	12	13	14	15
6	7	8	9	10
1	2	3	4	5

DOWNS

4TH E	WARM		80	81	82
3RD E	WARM		77	78	79
2ND E	COOL		24	25	26
	WARM		74	75	76
1ST E	COOL		21	22	23
	WARM		71	72	73

FRONT WASH

	SR	SL
(W1) BLUE	32	33
(W2) AMBER	30	31

(Amber & Blue = Magenta)

CYC SUBS
(Turn on electric non-dim!)

R	S12
G	S13
B	S14
A	S15

MISC

	SR	SL
FILL WASH	34	35
GOBOS	36	37

LADDERS

		SR	SL
4			
	TOP	44	49
	MID	54	59
	LOW	64	69
3			
	TOP	43	48
	MID	53	58
	LOW	63	68
2			
	TOP	42	47
	MID	52	57
	LOW	62	67
1			
	TOP	41	46
	MID	51	56
	LOW	61	66
GAL			
	TOP	40 Grn	45 Blu
	MID	50 Mag	55 Pnk
	LOW	60 Lav	65 Amb

SPECIALS

	SR	SL
CURTAIN GOBO		85
CYC GOBO	86	87
BREAK-UPS	36	37

SUBS

Another way to systematize your lights is to create "subs" (submasters) – which are groupings of lights that create a look, which are controlled by a master fader. They are called *sub*masters because they only control a certain amount of instruments, while the Grand Master is a fader on the light board that can bring up all the faders that are set, or completely blackout everything.

A lot of high school theatres are rented out to outside groups, and a lot of these groups are dance schools. In one district I worked in we had 10 dance schools that rented our two theatres, between one to three times a year each. We also had several jazz band and choir concerts a year, where we would create a mood for each tune with the lights. The concerts never held tech rehearsals. And while the dance companies (well, all but one) understood the value of a tech rehearsal, there was only one tech before a performance. Most dance schools don't have the time or money to create unique cues for each dance piece, which would take a significant amount of time and more than one tech rehearsal. Nor is it feasible to record cues for a most dance school recitals like you would do for a full-length play or musical, or even a full-length ballet, because there is usually no guarantee that what is rehearsed one day would actually be what was performed the next. So a quick and easy process is needed in order to quickly create looks for each dance, song or piece of music, which could be executed 'on the fly'.

This is where the subs on the light board come in very handy. The lighting designer can create a variety of looks – a jazzy amber look, a traditional ballet lavender look, a calm blue look, a hot red look, and various combination looks, and program these looks into the subs, so that a whole look can instantly be manually brought up with one fader.

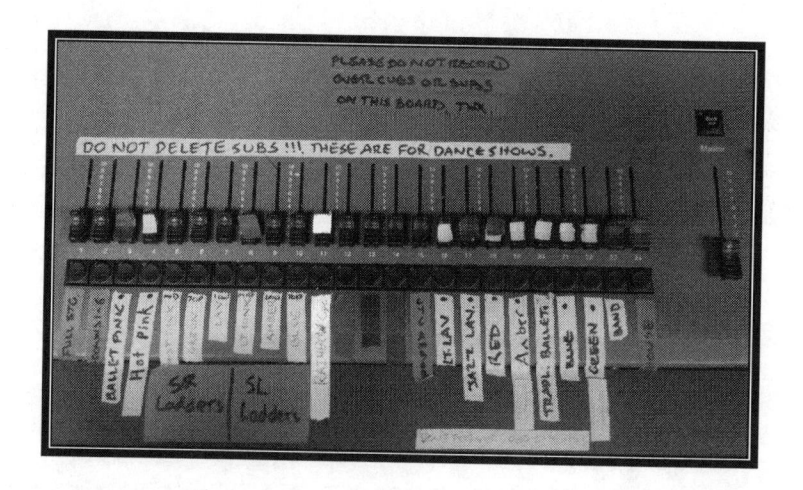

CHAPTER 7

TECH REHERSALS

In an ideal situation – particularly for full length plays and musicals, tech rehearsals are essential. Now it's time to put it all of the above planning into action. Having an understanding of the tech rehearsal process will also be a part of your arsenal, as it will help you design backwards.

THE START OF THE SHOW

Technical rehearsal (tech rehearsal for short) requirements vary from show to show. The purpose of tech rehearsals are so that the lighting technician can set the light levels and the timing of the cues, so that the sound technician knows when to play music or sound cues or when to bring up a mic level, so that the stage and rigging technicians know when to move a set piece in place or to raise or lower a drop or drape, and so that the actors can get used to working on the set, under the lights, with mics and sound, and with costumes and make-up (usually for the first time). The technicians and student crew need to do tech rehearsals so that they can learn the show. The actors have been practicing for weeks, so now it's the technician and crew's turn. They don't know the show like the actors do.

A strict rule of thumb I go by is to go in show-order whenever possible, and to conduct the rehearsal under show conditions. That means starting from the very beginning. Setting the house lights and the backstage lights, taking the house to half as if there was an audience there, taking the house lights out, opening the curtain, starting the first piece or act. I cannot count the number of times when a group has just started with their first act and not informed me and/or my technicians - they just start. We have to stop them and walk them through the start of show process. Shows don't just start like that, and if the performers and the technicians haven't practiced the start of the show during the tech, they are not going to know what to do in what order during the performance.

ROAD HOUSE

If a high school rents their theatre out to the community as well as hosts the schools in their district, as well as their own school, and they host a variety of events such as concerts, plays, meetings, dance recitals, variety shows, lectures, etc. then they are essentially operating as a "road house". There are three basic categories of events that come into a "road house". They are:

CATEGORY 1: CONCERTS/SPEAKERS

This category includes band concerts, choir concerts, lectures, meetings, school awards ceremonies and so on. These type of shows require minimal lighting – usually just a generic stage wash – where there are no light cues other than the house lights dimming at the start and raising at the end. There are no scenery or drapes that move during the show or event, and some are conducted entirely in front of the main curtain. The sound requirements may just be a mic or two, or fixed overheads, although for jazz band or choir there may be some solo mics needed. Because of these minimal requirements, although a Production Meeting is always in order, a tech rehearsal is not usually needed if everything is planned at the Production Meeting.

A word about jazz band and choir concerts. If I can, I like to move them into the Variety Show category. It is not traditional to have lighting changes during a classical concert, but I've found over the years that subtle lighting changes for a jazz concert –one cue for each piece - can enhance the mood of each piece. If a lighting designer is going to do lighting changes during a concert ideally it's best if she can hear each piece played or sung so she can adjust the light cues appropriately.

CATEGORY 2: VARIETY SHOWS AND DANCE RECITALS

When an outside variety show or dance recital comes into a high school theatre, they usually know that they need a tech rehearsal. The ones that sometimes need some convincing are school variety shows or talent shows. However, once they've run a show with a tech rehearsal the teacher will never go back, as they will see the benefits when their show runs more smoothly than it ever has done before.

Usually variety and dance shows hold one rehearsal. This is sufficient if you are just creating one look for each piece and if the sound and staging requirements are minimal and straightforward – the curtain is opened to reveal the dancers in place on stage, the CD starts playing, the light cue is brought up. A good rule of thumb is to:

allow two times the expected running length of the show for the tech rehearsal.

One steadfast rule for these types of shows with one tech rehearsal is, whenever possible go in show order. The fact that I've just said "steadfast rule" in the same sentence as "whenever possible", indicates the ideal verses the reality. Ideally the show will run a lot smoother if the performers and technicians have practiced it in order and know what is coming next after what has come before. However, particularly for these types of shows it is not always practical to have everyone there at the same time or to have people waiting around. As mentioned in the previous chapter, many dance recitals have over 100 students performing. Sometimes is makes sense to bring in all the young children first (who can be as young as two or three years old) and practice their dances and then let them go home to rest up for the evening's performance, even if in the show their dances are interspersed between other dances. This is not ideal and there is a greater chance of a performance being compromised, but as long as the technicians know this ahead of time they can compensate for it as best they can during the tech and performance.

It's a bit easier to do a dance recital out of order, but when a variety show requires a band's instruments being set up after a dance, which came after a skit that had a few set pieces that needed to move on and off, then it's more important to do the tech rehearsal in show order. Dragged out set changes can kill the flow and energy of the show for your audience. For this reason, during a Production Meeting, it's best for the lighting designer to encourage the event to alternate acts that are smaller that can go in front of the main curtains with acts that are larger or need more set up time. For instance, have a solo singer in front of the main curtain while a band strikes their instruments behind and a dance team gets in place. The curtains close on the band set up on stage, the solo singer sings, the curtains open on the dance team with an empty stage. The change in acts has run seamlessly for the audience.

CATEGORY 3: FULL LENGTH PLAYS AND MUSICALS

Full length performances must be carefully scheduled, and once the set is on stage the show should have exclusive use of the stage. For instance, a set cannot be moved to accommodate a band concert during the week. Let's talk about the schedule before we go into the actual tech rehearsal process.

In most of the high school theatres that I've worked in, all of which have functioned as road houses, time if of the essence, and each play loads in their set the weekend before tech rehearsals and loads it out the Sunday after a Saturday closing night. Some schools have the option – some would say "luxury" – of having a run through week on the set before tech week, and can take a few days following closing to strike the set and restore the rep plot. For our purposes here let's assume we have enough time – here's how a typical show schedule will look:

- Two weeks before tech – the lights are hung.

- Two Saturdays before tech week - the set is loaded in.

- Two Sundays before tech week – the lights are focused on the set.

- The week before tech week – run through for the cast on the set without lights or sound, sometimes with costumes.

- The Saturday before tech week – final touches on the set are made.

- The Sunday before tech week – dry tech, this usually takes about four to six hours depending on the show.
- Monday through Thursday - tech rehearsals through final dress, after school until about 10:00pm.
- Two or three weekends of performances.
- One "pick-up rehearsal" (this is a full tech) on the Wednesday or Thursday between the weekends.
- The Sunday or Monday after closing night – the set is struck.
- One day of the week following closing night – the lighting rep plot is restored.

This is quite a plush schedule. I have seen schools in districts that share a theatre at one school, where one set is loaded out and the next set is loaded in and the lights are hung and focused all on the Sunday following the first show's closing night on the Saturday and before the second show's first tech rehearsal on the Monday. Sometimes there is even a dry tech on the Sunday evening.

One last piece of the pie is if the show is a musical with an orchestra, and if your school has an orchestra pit cover that is supported by scaffolding (as opposed to a hydraulic lift). It can take about three hours for three to four technicians to remove and replace the pit cover each time, so you must also schedule this in.

HANGING AND FOCUSING THE LIGHTS

For full length plays and musicals time needs to be scheduled ahead of time for the designer and crew to hang and focus the lights. Many non-theatre people understand how much time it takes to build a set and sew costumes before tech week, but assume that the lighting is just a question of turning on a few switches. This couldn't be further from the truth. There is quite a bit of lighting preparation has to be done before the tech week starts.

If possible the light crew needs time on the stage alone in order to hang and focus the lights. The reason for this is that they need to be able to bring down electrics, move around the stage on a ladder or genie, and for focusing lights, ironically enough, they need the stage in almost complete darkness. There's also a lot of yelling going back and forth (unless you have a wireless headset system), and the crew needs to be able to hear each other. This is not a situation conducive to concurrently building or decorating sets, or holding rehearsals.

However, that said, this ideal is not always the reality of the time constraints inherent in high school theatre. Most experienced lighting and set crews are used to working around each other during tech. As long as a set crew is willing to work under less than ideal conditions during this time the light crew can hang and focus lighting while a set crew is working on stage. One caution is to warn a set crew about is that the stage may be going dark periodically. Because the set crew are working with hand tools and power tools, they must always be given a warning each time the stage has to go dark for the lighting crew.

Following is how much time one can expect to have to schedule for Hang and Focus. The times may vary depending on the experience of your light crew and how many "hands on deck", but this is a general rule for high school theatre.

Hanging, Circuiting, and Gelling Lights

Allow about 4 minutes per instrument.
For instance, if you have 60 instruments, you should schedule at least 4 hours for hanging.

Focusing Lights

Allow about 3 minutes per instrument.
For instance, if you have 60 instruments, you should schedule at least 3 hours for focusing.

TECH WEEK

Regardless of other time constraints or allowances, it's pretty standard for tech rehearsals to run Monday through Thursday (or through Wednesday with a Thursday opening) from right after school until about 10:00pm. Here's what to expect.

The Lighting Designer will ideally sit in the center of the house at the "Tech Table", with the Stage Manger and the Director. The Lighting Designer needs to see the lights as the audience would. The Lighting Designer and the Stage Manger will be in headset contact with the lighting technician at the light board, the sound technician at the sound board and the stage crew backstage (usually one person back stage has a headset and relays instructions to the rest of the crew). The Stage Manager will ask the actors to run through the show. The Lighting Designer will stop the cast in order to design and record cues, and to tell the Stage Manager when to call the cues, and to tell the lighting technician the timing of the cues. The light or sound board operators or the stage crew may need to practice the timing of a cue several times, and so the actors will have to run that part of the show over again. By dress rehearsal, the Stage Manager should be working together with all of the crew to execute the lighting and the designer's job is finished.

First Tech Rehearsal

This rehearsal is for the designers, Stage Manager and tech crew. The actors will have been rehearsing for 6 to 8 weeks, and now the tech need to set their "blocking and choreography". This will be a rehearsal with a lot of stopping, so the actors do a lot of standing around on stage and hanging around back stage during this time (a good opportunity to get homework done or study for tests!). This is no longer a time for the director to stop to give directions, nor a time for actors to go over scenes, although they often do. Each time this happens during a tech rehearsal it delays the process. Actors do not need to put on make-up or have finished costumes at this time.

For a Play

Tech rehearsals for a play usually take around two times the length of the play.
So, if a play is 2 hours long the first tech rehearsal will normally take 4 hours, in order to set the light levels and timing, and to practice set changes.

For a Musical

Tech rehearsals for a musical usually take around three times the length of the musical.
So, if a musical is 2 hours long the first tech rehearsal will normally take 6 hours, in order to set the light levels and timing, and to practice set changes. Some directors choose to do this over the course of two days; Act I the first day, Act II the next.

Second Tech Rehearsal

Again, the actors have been rehearsing for many weeks, and now it is the tech crew's turn to rehearse their parts. The tech crew has now received their "blocking and choreography". The designers now need to refine their cues, and the tech crew need to "rehearse" executing their cues. Again, this will be a rehearsal with a lot of stopping, and sometime sections of the play will have to be repeated in order to get the timing correct on light cues, set changes, etc. It's best to have full costumes at this time, but make-up is not necessary.

The second tech rehearsal may go a bit quicker than the first, but not always.

Set Change Rehearsal

Usually around this time the set crew have the stage to themselves for a couple of hours before the Third Tech Rehearsal, in order to rehearse their set changes. A slow and awkward set change can kill the energy of a show. Set crews should be able to do the set change quickly, yet also safely. For instance, they should not run, but they shouldn't amble about either. They should be walking "with purpose", and each crew member should know what their job is for each set change. This takes some practice and should not be done under the added stress of actors moving about and lights and sound cues happening.

Third Tech Rehearsal

Not many schools and companies have the luxury of a third tech rehearsal, or some schools may decide to open their show a day early, or have an 'invitational dress', but if there is time, this should be a rehearsal with minimal stopping, while the crew practices their light cues and set moves in 'real time' as much as possible. Full costumes and make-up are a good idea by this point.

Final Dress Rehearsal

This is where it all comes together, regardless of how many tech rehearsals have preceded this day. The crews should know their light and sound cueing and set movements, and the actors should be in full costume and make-up. This rehearsal should be under performance conditions, and there should be no stopping for any reason. The director and designers can take notes during the rehearsal and make any refinements and/or changes after each act.

Between Techs

It's also important, if possible, for there to be time allotted between the tech rehearsals for the crews to make adjustments. For instance, it may become obvious during a tech rehearsal that a light, or several lights, are the wrong gel color, the wrong focus, or in the wrong place. Or, extra lights may need to be hung, gelled and focused that weren't anticipated during the run-throughs. Sound technicians may discover they need to add another mic into the set, or that a monitor needs to be moved. The set crew may need to re-spike a set piece, and so on. This is what tech rehearsals are for, so there is nothing wrong with this, but the need for extra time should be anticipated and scheduled. There is no point holding all the actors while adjustments such as these are done by the crews.

DRY TECH

A Dry Tech is where the Lighting Designer, the Stage Manager, the technician operating the light board and the Director sit down together and design and record preliminary cuing without actors on stage. Set pieces need to be moved into place to set cues for each scene, so the set crew should be in attendance too. Adjustments can made to take into account the actor's and set's actual movement during the First Tech Rehearsal.

Although Dry Techs are not imperative, if there is time for a Dry Tech before the First Tech Rehearsal, this will make the whole tech process run more quickly and smoothly for the actors, as adjustments take less time than initial designing.

THE DESIGN PROCESS

So, what is the lighting designer's role in all this? What process does the lighting designer go through in order to use all of this information to design a play?

Following is roughly the process that a lighting designer goes through. It's not always in this order, and it may include other steps, or it may not include all of these steps, but the process is fairly universal. So, here we go...

OBTAIN A COPY OF THE SCRIPT
- Perform a script analysis Read the script. Note possible cues, black outs, etc. that dialog and stage directions in the script call for.

MEET WITH THE DIRECTOR
- Meet with the Director to discuss his/her concepts and visions for the play.

WATCH A RUN THROUGH REHEARSAL
- Make notes in the script (in pencil!) of possible cues and blackouts.
- Think about:
  - Location: inside, outside, in a living room, in a circus tent, in the forest, on the street?
  - Time(s) of day (what color is the light, from what angle does it come).
  - Do you need specials: where do the actors move, does one or more actors or a part of the set need to be isolated, is there a dream sequence or other motivation for non-realistic lighting?
  - When do the cues happen, how fast should they happen; a slow fade or a bump. What is the motivation for each cue.
  - How bright should each individual area, special and/or cue be.
  - Where (from what angle) should the light come from; what is the motivating factor?
  - What color should the light be and why: what color is the light in a forest, in a living room, in an office. (Start to notice these things in your daily life.)

DRAFT THE PLOT
- Make several copies of your light plot (always keep an original).
- Think about all the instruments you will need to achieve the above objectives.
- Hand draw the instruments onto a copy of your light plot.
- Make adjustments and compensations for dimmer and circuit capacity and instrument inventory.
- Draft light plot using lighting template and proper drafting procedures.
- Make at least two copies of your plot for hang and focus, keep your original elsewhere.

WRITE UP PATCH SCHEDULE AND DIMMER SCHEDULE
- Transfer the information on your light plot to your patch schedule and dimmer schedule; area or special, dimmer number, circuit number, number of instruments, gel color, etc.
- Make at least two copies of your schedules for hang and focus and for your script binder, keep your original elsewhere.

HANG AND FOCUS
- Hang the lights as per your plot, and call the focus.

FIRST TECH REHEARSAL
- Design each cue as the actors run through the play.
- This rehearsal is for you, not for the actors, so feel free to stop them at any time in order to get a cue designed and recorded.
- If it's done right the first time, it will speed up subsequent techs.
- The Board Operator records what each cue is on his/her cue sheets or on the computer, and the Stage Manager records when each cue happens on his/her script.
- Allow about two times the expected length of the play for this first tech rehearsal (sometimes more!).
- Each cue should be numbered in sequence.
- The cues for the beginning of the show and the beginning of intermission should run roughly as follows:
  - Set a pre-show or intermission "scene" (cue 0).
  - House to half (cue 1). (This warns the audience that it's time to be seated.)
  - House out and blackout) (cue 2).
  - Stage lights up (cue 3).

RE-DRAFT AND RE-HANG
- Sometimes it is necessary to move, add, or delete some instruments.
- Re-draft your plot, re-write your schedules, re-hang and/or re-focus.

TECHS AND DRESS REHEARSALS
- Make adjustments to your cues (the look and the timing) as you see fit.
- The Stage Manager should add Standby's (and Warnings as needed) in his/her script.
- Have the Stage Manager and crew follow the Pre- and Post-Show checklist for all techs and performances.

ATTEND OPENING NIGHT
- Attend the opening night as an audience member to make sure everything is running smoothly.

THEORY TO REALITY

Of course, all this theory about tech rehearsals helping you to design backwards is only theory. The best thing to do is to find yourself a local high school to volunteer at, where you can be a part of the process from the hang and focus to opening night. That's the only way to really understand how the design choice you make while drafting impact the end users.

CHAPTER 8

LET'S BEGIN DESIGNING A LIGHTING SYSTEM

Now that you've been working backwards from the end user, we can start to make some initial decisions. The primary decisions an architect makes that affects how a lighting designer can do their job is the placement of the lighting positions and the count and configuration of the circuits at the lighting positions.

We will primarily be talking about proscenium theatres in this section.

LIGHTING POSITIONS

CATWALKS/BEAMS

Let's start with the catwalks. You may be installing catwalks or beams in your theatre. Catwalks hang below the ceiling while beams are installed above the ceiling. The look and the access is different, but they all serve the same purpose as front of house lighting, so for our purposes here I will just refer to all front of house positions as catwalks.

How many catwalks do you need? This is where designing backwards comes into play. The answer is - it depends on the size of the stage. In this case, specifically the depth of the stage. By designing backwards, you can avoid the problem Jo came across in her theatre with the actors' eyes being in shadow. There was little Jo could do about that problem, because it wasn't an issue with how the lighting instruments had been set, it was an issue with the placement of the catwalks in the building.

As we discussed before the optimal angle to light an actors face is from 45 degrees from above. Using McCandless, the stage is typically divided up into 8' circles called "acting areas". The first "zone" of acting areas typically covers the apron. Depending on the size of your stage there may be four to six acting areas across the apron.

On your plans, draw a 6' actor standing in the center of one of these acting areas. Now, in your section view draw a line at a 45 degree angle from a level 6' plane above the stage deck. In other words, from the actor's face to the height where you have determined your catwalks will be (or to the beams above the house ceiling).

This is where you should place your furthest catwalk from the stage – called the 3rd catwalk.

The second zone of acting areas typically falls somewhere under the proscenium arch, depending on the size of the apron that you have to light. Repeat the process above, using a 45 degree angle emanating from 6' above the stage deck to the catwalk level to determine how far away from the stage to place the second catwalk.

The third zone is where it gets tricky. The third zone of acting areas are typically just upstage of the proscenium. If you light these areas from a catwalk at 45 degrees you have to make sure that the angle of the light doesn't light the top of the proscenium arch instead. If you light these areas from the first electric the angle is generally too steep and causes dark shadows on the actors' faces. The only thing you can do in this case is to draw a section view of the stage, divide the stage into the areas, decide on the best placement for the first catwalk and make sure your proscenium (and the boarders/teasers) will be high enough for the light to have a straight shot to light the actor's faces. Remember, too, that it's not just an actor standing in the center of an acting area that has to be lit, the areas need to blend into each other, so you must also determine how far upstage the actor can walk before he is lit by the first electric without a dark line in between.

It's also important to have a catwalk above the apron. Above the stage deck upstage of the proscenium down lights can be hung on the electrics, but I've seen too many school theatres with no option o hang down lights above the apron in front of the proscenium, so when an actor walks from upstage to downstage the lighting on them flattens out because suddenly there is no down lighting.

Three is usually the maximum number of catwalks needed, and it would be the ideal amount in most high school theatres, which typically have 400 to 1000 seats in the house. Again, it depends entirely on designing backwards, depending on the size of the stage.

Sometimes a compromise has to be made, especially in school theatres – usually because of budget. It may not be possible to have three catwalks so the first two zones have to be lit from the second catwalk. If this will be the case in your theatre place the second catwalk in between the 45 degree angles from the first and second acting area zones. Generally the lighting instruments used to light the first zone from the second catwalk would have a smaller beam angle than the instruments used to light the second zone from the second catwalk, because the throw is further.

The length of the catwalks is also determined by McCandless theory. The catwalks should not end at the edge of the stage. They need to extend far enough past the end of the sides of the stage so that the outermost lighting instrument can light the outermost acting area from an angle of 45 degrees in plan view as well as in section.

Regardless of how many, catwalks are typically numbered from the proscenium arch. Therefore the closest catwalk to the stage is catwalk #1. Catwalk #2 is the next one. Catwalk #3 would be the furthest from the stage.

ELECTRICS

Electrics hung above the stage should be spaced approximately 7' to 8" apart. Generally a 30' to 40' deep stage (from the proscenium) needs four electrics. The first electric should be as close to the proscenium as possible, allowing for the main (sometimes called: grand) curtain, any projection screen and the first border (sometimes called: teaser). This is because the area lighting from this position shouldn't be at too steep an angle.

Electrics are also typically numbered from the proscenium arch. Therefore the closest electric from the front of the stage is electric #1. Electric #2 is the next electric upstage of that. That makes electric #1 just upstage of the proscenium and catwalk #1 just downstage of the proscenium.

LADDERS

Ladders are a type of electric that run from downstage to upstage at the sides of the stage. Typically the electric runs above and bars hang down from them so that the lights can shine between each leg. There are usually four sets of ladders on each electric in a theatre that has four electrics.

Ladders can be used to hang high-side instruments on, but the primary purpose of having lights on the ladders is for dance lighting in ballets, dance recitals and musicals. As you will remember, in dance we want to light the body, not so much the face. For this reason the lowest part of the ladder should be able to be lowered to about 1' to 18" off the stage deck. When an instrument is this low it is called a "shin buster" - for good reason.

Don't scrimp on the ladder budget. High school theatres - which increasingly act as road houses with their own productions, district productions and outside productions – have many events that call for side lighting. If there are no ladders in the theatre, the lighting crew spends a lot of time trying to create them. They do this either by hanging pipes on the end of electrics, which entails running lots of cables, or by setting booms on the stage on which to hang instruments, which also entails running lots of cables, but this time across the stage floor. Pipes hanging down from the electrics, or booms set on the stage deck, also cannot be moved for set changes the way that ladders can be independently, and easily flown.

GALLERIES /BOX BOOMS

It seems to be the trend these days to provide theatres with galleries at the front of the house instead of box booms. Galleries are built on the outside of the wall, such that they are visible to the audience, whereas box booms can be (not always) recessed into the wall. The benefit of galleries is that they are generally more easily accessible and there is more space to hang more instruments. The benefit to box booms is that they can be recessed into the wall and hide the instruments from the audience's view.

The decision on whether to design galleries or box booms is personal preference. I prefer the option of being able to hang more instruments on galleries. When designing galleries be sure to make them straight. Rounded galleries make the half of the gallery furthest from the stage inoperational because you can't get a straight shot to the stage as you're shooting around a corner.

Another use for galleries is to extend the ladder lighting out to the proscenium. If a stage has side lighting from the ladders, these only cover the part of the stage deck upstage of the proscenium. As soon as an actor or dancer steps downstage of the proscenium onto the apron the effect is lost. By hanging instruments on the galleries just downstage of the proscenium wall, in the house, in the same configuration, and at the same height you primarily use your ladder lighting, it continues the effect to the whole stage.

FLOOR POCKET AND WALL OUTLETS

In theatres without ladders, where floor booms are used, floor pockets are often placed in between each leg to provide a place to plug in the cables.

Floor pockets can also be used to plug in "practicals". Practicals are "real life" fixtures that are built into a set, such as a table lamp or a street light, that need to be controlled at the light board in order to time their fade up or down with a cue. Practicals usually come with Edison plugs, so these need to be plugged into an adapter that plugs into the theatre's lighting cable, which then can be plugged into the floor pocket by the stage technician who moves the set piece into place.

Wall outlets are also useful for practicals that are further upstage. They are also useful for any uplighting on the cyc.

ORCHESTRA PIT CIRCUITS

I've often seen lighting circuits placed in orchestra pits. This may seem counterintuitive, unless you're a lighting designer who likes to up-light from the pit – much to the conductor and orchestra's chagrin. But, there are legitimate reasons to do this. I once designed the lighting for a show that had two characters sitting on a bridge about a river. I was able to put an instrument in the pit with a gobo rotator and a light blue gel, so that it looked like the reflection of the water shining up onto the underneath side of the bridge and the characters.

HOW MANY CIRCUITS

Let's design backwards by looking at what a lighting designer will want to light so that the number of circuits to provide can be determined.

I rarely see an insufficient amount of circuits on electrics. Circuits placed on 15" - 18" centers across an electric are usually sufficient. Remember to extend your circuits to the end of the electrics far enough to be able to light someone standing on the same side of the stage from a 45 degree angle from the side.

Catwalks is where I typically see a woeful amount of circuits. In three school theatres build in the early 2000's that I worked in, which were designed by the same theatre consultant, there were only 10 circuits on the second catwalk and 20 on the first catwalk. The first catwalk was just about sufficient, but the second catwalk was completely inadequate.

Let's look at how many circuits you need on a second catwalk in a theatre with two catwalks. The ideal is to use the McCandless method and light each acting area with two instruments from 45 degrees in plan view and section view. Using a common proscenium opening of 40', let's say our stage will have 5 acting areas across. That means in order to light the first zone of acting areas alone you would need 10 circuits.

The next most common effect to light from the catwalks is the front color washes. The option of three washes is the most functional. Usually the washes come from the second catwalk in a two-catwalk theatre. But the determining factor is again reached by designing backwards. Let's look at the end result of the wash effect. The wash is a light that comes in at a low angle and flattens out the actors and set; fairly diffuse with few shadows. The wash should also wash the whole stage from the edge of the apron all the way upstage to the cyc. Here's the problem with washes though. If you have them at too low of an angle, they light halfway up the cyc and create a line about 6' or 8' up the cyc because of where the proscenium arch stops the light. If for instance you are using blue cyc lights with an amber wash, the top half of your cyc will be blue and the bottom half will be amber. To avoid this we normally use the shutters in the instrument and shutter the light off the cyc. But this means that because of the angle the light is coming from, if you shutter it off the bottom of the cyc – at stage deck level – a 6' actor standing next to the cyc will not be lit by the wash, only his feet will be lit. If that actor walks forward (down stage) he will need to walk several feet away from the cyc before he is lit by the wash lights, leaving the upstage section of the stage unusable. Of course, wash lights coming in from a steeper angle would help alleviate this problem.

When I asked the theatre consultant, who had designed the three 2000-decade theatres, the reason for only ten circuits on his second beam he explained his reasoning to me. He typically used the first beam for washing the downstage half of the stage, and would wash the upstage half of the stage from the first electric. A fair enough design choice. However, this would require twice as many instruments, which his lighting packages didn't allow for because of the schools' budget constraints. Nor had he changed his circuit plan to reflect this on the first electric, which usually has to have the capacity to handle areas, washes, high sides and any specials. Luckily at his third theatre I had come in during the construction phase. By the time I came on board it was too late to have more circuits added, but we were able to do a bit of re-wiring so that there were more circuits allocated to the second beam, which allowed for the wash effect from the second beam with the instruments that were available.

As you can see, it's often a case of juggling. But making architectural decisions without first having made the decisions a lighting designer would make creates problems for the end user for the life of the building. Designing backwards is essential.

So back to our question of how many circuits to put on the second catwalk in a two-catwalk theatre. We've determined that there will be five acting areas with two lights each, so there's 10 circuits right there. It's best to have four instruments per wash for intensity purposes, but three can suffice. With four instruments you have the option of splitting the stage in half and washing only stage right or stage left. With three instruments you also have a center stage option, but lose intensity. In an ideal world, five instruments per wash would be nice. But for our purposes lets assume we're on a budget and plan for three instruments for a wash. With three washes, that's a total of nine instruments, and therefore a total of nine circuits. So now we're up to 19 circuits with just one zone of areas and a basic wash.

But remember, in our two catwalk scenario, we need to light two acting area zones from the second catwalk as well, so that's another 10 circuits, bringing us to a total of 29 circuits so far. Then, we have to allow for any specials each show will dictate. These can include break-up gobos, center specials, and so on. Plus you have to allow room for the followspots – typically on the second beam as well - to move between the instruments. Let's throw in another six to 10 circuits.

So, 36 circuits on a second catwalk, in a two catwalk-theatre, is not uncalled for.

There is another method of lighting the stage called the Broadway method. This is typically used for musicals. The primary difference is the use of one instrument per acting area (actually, acting areas don't come into play per se, but we'll call it that for our purposes). The single instrument is aimed straight at the acting area from the front, which has the effect of flattening facial features. This isn't ideal, but it doesn't come into play too much when using the Broadway method, because there is a lot of lighting from the sides and top that comes into play. Designing a theatre system for this method of lighting the stage requires just as much backwards designing as for any method.

What commonly happens in school theatres is that because of budget constraints the school is able to purchase only one instrument per acting area –creating a combined McCandless-Broadway method. If this is the case in a school theatre that you are designing, then you will only need one circuit per acting area. In our scenario, this would cut down the need for 10 circuits, so in that case 26 circuits on the second electric would be sufficient. But, without knowing what the school's budget is and what lighting method they will be using in the theatre, the amount of circuits to spec can't be determined.

In the case of how many circuits to put on the electrics we also have down lights to consider. I've seen red, green, blue "Multi-PARs", and I've seen a warm and cool down light assigned to each area. I've also seen a set of down lights and a set of back lights. In general, the number of circuits I've seen on electrics hasn't been too much of a problem. But, it always seems they are a few short – particularly on the downstage electrics where more specials tend to get hung, including gobos for the cyc - so I can't say there is always not enough. But often times - there is not enough. Again, designing backwards will resolve this issue for the life of the theatre.

In the case of floor pockets and wall circuits I've normally seen the opposite – more circuits than is needed. But if the budget allows, put them in anyway as it allows for greater flexibility, a lower cable budget and a lower gaff tape budget. Flexibility is a theatre technician's friend.

NUMBERING CIRCUITS

Even if there are enough actual circuits, I've seen numbering systems reduce the usable amount of circuits in half. I often seen circuit numbers doubled in high school theatres. Either numbered along the electrics 1 1 2 2 3 3 4 4 5 5 and so on, or 1 2 3 4 5... 1 2 3 4 5... There are schools of thought behind these choices - but don't do it. Numbering circuits in these ways makes assumptions that the lighting designers who come into the space will want to put their instruments only in those configurations. Circuits numbered simply 1, 2, 3, 4, 5, 6, 7, 8, 9, 10.... is more widely needed.

Another circuit numbering system I've seen is on the electric where the cyc lights are planned to be hung. The circuits are sometimes ganged in threes to allow for red, green, blue cyc configurations. However, that's assuming that the set designer will always want the cyc in that position. I once worked in a school district that had two high school theatres. It suited one school to have their cyc upstage of the third electric and the other school to have their cyc upstage of the fourth electric. Occasionally, because of certain set designs, or because of certain events (such as a full orchestra) we would move the cyc and consequently have to move all the cyc lights. This made circuiting the single instruments, which were then put on what was the cyc electric, difficult, as there wasn't always a circuit above an instrument. It's best to number the circuits individually and leave the decision of what to put where up to the lighting designers who will use the space – allow for versatility.

Another circuiting configuration that I see frequently is on the ladders. It is assumed that there will be two instruments of three colors on each ladder, so typically three doubled circuits are put on each ladder. However, this doesn't allow for the option of hanging any specials on the ladders. In one high school theatre I worked in the budget didn't allow for doubled instruments on the ladders, so there was only one instrument for each of the three colors on each ladder provided in the lighting package. At times there were occasions where it would have been appropriate to hang an instrument as a special on a ladder, because there was certainly enough room, but because the circuits provided were doubled and not singles there was no power to do so.

This doubling up of circuits is also common on galleries. In short, number all of your circuits individually, because it provides the Lighting Designer with more flexibility and saves on the cable and labor budgets in the long run.

CHAPTER 9

TIPS FOR DESIGNING BLACK BOX THEATRES

A black box theatre has a high versatility factor; it can be re-configured to a proscenium stage, a thrust stage or theatre-in-the-round. But, with versatility comes expenses. Each time the acting space is reconfigured the lighting instruments and drapes have to be moved to new positions. Most high schools don't have the budget for the labor that this versatility requires nor the amount of instruments it requires. The costs take the administration by surprise, and the time requirements take the drama teacher by surprise, as it takes too long than she has in class with the students to be reconfiguring the space. With no time and no money the space soon loses its versatility.

For instance, one school I worked at had a black box theatre and they hired me to create a lighting rep plot for them. Theatre-in-the-round and thrust stages require about twice the number of lighting instruments than a proscenium stage does because the actors and the sets must be lit from several sides. This theatre had been given a lighting package, but it was insufficient for the space potential, and the tech theatre class time was limited, so the Drama teacher decided to create a fixed proscenium stage within the black box space with flats as the proscenium walls.

In another black box school theatre I worked there were an ample amount of instruments but there were no lighting positions to allow for lighting the stage from the sides. There were plenty of pipes and electrics over where the stage deck normally was placed but they did not extend over the side-audience positions, so that there was no way to light the actors from the sides of the stage except from above. So we had no choice but to structure the theatre into a permanent proscenium configuration too. If you are going to design a black box theatre for a high school campus, keep in mind that users will want to maximize the space, including extending a stage deck as far to the walls as possible. Because you never know what configuration the users of a black box theatre want to use, be sure that your pipes and electrics extend all the way to all the walls.

On the other hand, there are some benefits to a black box theatre. For instance, a black box theatre's floor space can be cleared for classes and rehearsals to be held in there. A black box theatre is great for learning environments where tech theatre skills – particularly stage lighting - are a part of the curriculum. For instance, lighting techniques can be taught during a composition class, where the students hang and focus the lighting and create cues to a piece of music. A black box theatre is more suited to a college or a university, which will have a technical theatre degree program, than to a high school, which has more budgetary and time constraints.

In most cases, however, it is perhaps better to provide high schools with a small 100-seat proscenium theatre. In the two examples above, had the administration assessed future operations, budget and time restrictions ahead of time, money would not have been wasted on building this type of space that was never going to be used for its intended purposes.

PART 2

OTHER STUFF

CHAPTER 10

WORK LIGHTS

A whole chapter must be devoted to work lights. Although they are not involved in performance lighting design, chances are if you are spec'ing production lights you also are charged with spec'ing the work lights.

There are two basic types of lighting systems in the theatre; production lights and work lights. Production lights are the ellipsoidals/lekos, fresnels, PARs, cycs, etc, which are used to light everything from a principal addressing students to a full musical production. This is the light that enables audiences to see performers and presenters. These lights have lamps that have a relatively short lamp life and can cost at least $15 each to replace, some much more. Most of these lamps consume 500 to 1,000 watts of power each, and therefore are expensive to run. They cause a lot of heat and therefore increase HVAC costs. In addition these lamps are almost never used without a color filter, or "gel". Gels burn out fairly regularly (meaning their color fades, or a hole is literally burned in the middle of the material), so there is the expense of replacing gels too. For these reasons, production lights must be "saved" (turned off whenever they are not in use) in order to get the best use out of them for the least amount of money. Any person who is in charge of a theatre budget will attest to the importance of "saving the lights" when not in use.

What the audience doesn't see is the times when the work lights are in use. The purpose of work lights, as you can guess, is to light work. Work set building, work hanging production lights, work rehearsing, work doing rigging, work choreographing, and class work. These lights, while needing to be bright enough for the work being done, do not need to create mood and location. They are purely for functional reasons.

Work lights usually house one of four main types of "lamps" (light bulbs).

>Incandescent – like your standard household lamp. The favorite to our eye, because historically and psychologically we are used to a 'black burning body' as a light source (think cavemen sitting around a fire at night and in the sunshine during the day).

Fluorescent – better efficacy (more light for the amount of power being used) than incandescents. Awful color, but they last longer than incandescents, and are therefore cheaper to run.

HID – High Intensity Discharge – far better efficacy than either of the above, and they last longer, but they can take ten to twenty minutes to warm up, and hence are not very practical (particularly if there was an emergency situation that required instant illumination). They also make people look like they're not feeling too well.

LED – Light Emitting Diodes – fast becoming the industry standard for work lights, due to the fact that their efficacy is so good, they don't need replacing very often, the color isn't too bad, and they can instantly be switched on and off.

THE TROUBLE IS...

The trouble is, that many a high school theatre is ill equipped with work lights. Even in high school theatres that have work lights they are often under utilized. In many older theatres they may have been added as an after thought, or sometimes not at all. For this reason, teachers or others working in the theatre will turn on the whole production lighting system in order to light their classes, rehearsals and set building sessions. In one theatre I worked at I figured this amount to equal about 44,000 watts of power being used. In another theatre with a more extensive production lighting system, with no theatre management to stop them from turning on every single production light when working in the theatre, I calculated that they were using about 120,000 watts of power!

In many newer theatres the situation isn't much better. In another theatre I worked at, which had the misfortune to be built in 2008 during the recession, because of budget cuts at the time of installation, work lights were eliminated from the equipment order all together. There were fluorescent overheads installed 40' up at the grid, but these were too far away to be of much use, and no one wanted to use them too much because it would be very difficult to replace the lamps once they burned out. Therefore the classes, rehearsals and set builders turned on most of the production lights in order to be able to see well enough to work in the space. I hate to think how much has been spent in power over the years, just in order to save a bit of money on an initial purchase of necessary equipment (circuitry was installed, the instruments were just never purchased).

If you are designing a theatre or managing a theatre that needs to install new work lights you will be able to compare initial costs with running costs and figure out what is the best choice of equipment. I personally prefer LEDs. They can be more expensive per fixture, but the long-term financial and functional benefits far outweigh the initial costs.

WHY LED WORK LIGHTS?

Most of the technical theatre people that I've worked with vastly prefer that LED fixtures be used for work lights. The primary reason is that they turn on and off instantly, with no warm up time. Also, if they are installed on the electrics then they are easy to get to should the lamps ever need replacing, or should the fixtures ever need repair. Incandescent and fluorescent fixtures would also be great work lights because they can turn on and off instantly, however they have such a short lamp life, and get so hot, that financially they are impractical to use for something that is going to be on a lot of the time. HID fixtures have a very long lamp life and therefore one would think would be the most practical to use for work lights, but they also have such a long warm up time (and an even longer warm up time if you turn them off and suddenly realize you need to turn them on again) that they are very impractical in a theatre situation. As happened in one theatre I worked at, the warm up time was too long, so people would get impatient and turn on the production lights, which only has the effect of increasing the budget – something one was trying to avoid by installing the worklights in the first place.

WORK LIGHTS POLICY

No matter what work light system you design for your high school theatre, encourage the school administration to develop a policy for the use of the work lights and production lights. Here is a sample policy I wrote for a high school that had HID lights on the electrics and above the apron of the stage, fluorescent lights on the grid, and a limited amount of production lights programmed into an auto control to provide a few basic production functions.

SAMPLE PRODUCTION LIGHTS AND WORK LIGHTS USE POLICY

All rehearsals, classes and set building should be conducted with work lights only.

There are work lights on all the electrics and on the apron. These are to be used for anything other than actual tech rehearsals or performances. These have a warm up time, but they are plenty bright once they've warmed up.

The lights marked "Stage Overheads" should be used as little as possible.

These are the fluorescents up above the cables for the fly system. Because these will be difficult to re-lamp, only use these in the case of an emergency when you need light instantly.

For productions requiring only a neutral stage wash and no cuing, use the auto preset faders on the SM Panel.

The preset panel has certain "looks" recorded, and the faders are labeled as such. These are sufficient for school-day assemblies, etc.

Use of the light board.

If you feel there is a need to turn on the light board for any reason, please contact the Theatre Manager ahead of time, and a lighting technician can be scheduled for your show. Please do not use the light board without a technician supervising. (In the past, light cues for a large production - that took several days to program, involving many people - were almost deleted by two students who were unattended and were trying to re-record the cues for a school day event.)

When vacating the theatre, please turn out all lights except for the Night Light.

CHAPTER 11

HEADSETS

This chapter on communication headset systems is included in this book because they are one of the most important systems you will spec in a theatre to make lighting any event or production run smoothly.

Headsets are a vital element of designing stage lighting. Without headsets the lighting designer cannot communicate to the light board operator and followspot operators during the tech rehearsal, and the stage manager can't tell the lighting operators when to take their cues during the show.

You will hear of two types of headsets spoken about around a theatre. One type belongs to the theatre's communication system that the crew uses, the other kind are mics that performers wear. Usually if you just hear the term "headset" we are talking about the communication system. Also, you will hear the whole arrangement, which includes the headset, beltpack and cables referred to as "the headset". Technically the beltpack carries the power and the headset itself is plugged into it, but we call the whole thing "the headset". When a Stage Manager tells her crew to "set up the headsets" she means to plug in or put in place the headsets, cables and beltpacks.

Headsets are a priority item for lighting a production. Recommend to your school's administrators to get the best brand money can buy, but if you can't shift their budget to purchase even an inexpensive headset system, at least find some way so that their crews can communicate to each other. I've worked with walkie talkies, lately cell phones, even a baby monitor. Yes, it's true. In one theatre we did not have any headsets for the followspot operators up in the catwalks, so I brought in an old baby monitor that I had a home. We put the receiver (the end parents would have with them) by the followspot operators and I held the transmitter (the end that would go in the baby's room). That way I could talk to the followspot ops and relay cues to them and they could hear me. Of course they couldn't talk to me, but I could tell each time they received my commands by the correct adjustments made to the followspot light. Find something to spec that works; the smooth operation of every show, not matter how small, depends on communication between crew members.

HOW MANY HEADSETS JACKS AND WHERE?

How many headsets positions should you spec in a new theatre or how many headsets should you purchase for an existing theatre? It never ceases to amaze me that multi-million dollar, state-of-the-art high school theatres are provided with two to four jacks to plug in headsets and that's it, or the theatre is built with enough jacks, but is stocked with just a few headsets.

The very minimum I recommend is 8 jacks. Here are the locations where you should spec a headset jack:

1. In the booth where the Stage Manager will sit to call the light cues and indeed the whole a show.

2. In the booth where the Light Board Operator will sit to run the light board.

3. At the sound board (which you've put in the house).

4. At the position where the first followspot is placed.

5. At the position where the second followspot is placed. (Even if the followspots are together, each operator needs his or her own headset, or else one followspot will lag behind the other if "Go's" have to be relayed.)

6. Stage right. This headset jack should be near the fly rail if it's on that side of the stage and should not be placed such that the technician wearing it will drape the cable across a doorway or the path of an entering or exiting actor. Plan ahead for where a crew member is likely to be standing, whether it's a rigger operating the fly rail or a Stage Manager who is calling the show from back stage. Or both.

7. Stage left, or the side of the stage opposite the fly rail. Likewise with stage left, think about what the technician needs access to and whether the cable will be in the way of actors making entrances and exits, and stage crew moving set pieces.

8. A jack in the floor at the center of the house where the Lighting Designer will sit to design the show. It's actually best to have two jacks at that position because the Stage Manager should be sitting at the tech table for the first few days of tech next to the Lighting Designer so that they can more easily confer on cues during the tech.

As you can see it would be impossible for the light crew and to communicate with the other crew members without a sufficient headset system installed in their theatre.

OTHER HEADSET POSITIONS TO CONSIDER

ORCHESTRA PIT

Will your theatre have an orchestra pit? If so, the Stage Manger will need to communicate with the Conductor. The Conductor will not wear the headset during the show, because he or she has to hear the music. But it is useful to be able to communicate with the pit in order to let the Conductor know when to start the overture or the entre-acte, when a cue comes up that needs special notification because the Conductor can't see what is going on, or in case of an emergency where the Conductor needs to talk to the Stage Manager or the reverse.

BOX OFFICE

The Stage Manager needs to communicate with the House Manager about when to start the show, because the Stage Manager must be in her place ten minutes before the show starts, making sure that the actors and crew are ready. If the Stage Manager cannot communicate with the House Manager, the Stage Manager may start the show when her crew and the actors are ready, but there may still be a line of audience members in the lobby still waiting to get into the house. It would be inconvenient, if not unsafe, to black out the house before all of the audience is seated. The House Manager needs to be able to inform the Stage Manager to hold the show if there are still audience members arriving.

DRESSING ROOMS/GREEN ROOM/WAITING ROOMS

It's not a good idea to let performers have access to the crew's communication system – too many cooks… But, for a large show, a Stage Manager may need to communicate with a crew member who has been placed backstage (when I say "backstage" in this case, I mean out of the stage space, not in the wings – the term is somewhat interchangeable and depends on the context of the situation).

SCENE SHOP AND COSTUME SHOP

Another reason it might be a good idea to have a headset backstage would be for a costumer to communicate to the Stage Manager in case there was a problem with a costume, which might require delaying the start of a show, or stalling a scene change. If the budget allows, it's also good to have the option for someone to plug in a headset in the scene shop, although that location is primarily used before the show has opened, not during the running of a show. Only in extenuating circumstances would set building – most likely a repair of some sort - be going on during a show. Some scene shops are used for set storage during a show.

EXTRA JACKS IN THE WINGS

Again, if the budget allows, place at least one extra headset jack on stage right and one extra on stage left. If you already have jacks down stage, consider placing extras up stage, or in the middle of the rail. That way two crew members aren't plugged in at the same place and daisy chained (see next section) together, and won't trip over each other's cables.

LOADING BRIDGE

The loading bridge isn't used during a show, but it is used for re-weighting when hanging lights or scenery. Do not install a headset jack up there. Use a wireless headset, and if a wireless headset is not available crew can shout to each other. Better to go hoarse than to trip over a cable and fall to your death.

DAISY-CHAINING

Most wired headset beltpacks have the capacity to plug one headset beltpack into another in a "daisy chain" configuration, sometimes called "piggy-backing". (If not, don't spec or purchase that brand of headsets, because this option offers a lot of versatility.) The beltpack has three holes. One is for the cable that is plugged into the wall jack, which provides the belt pack with its power and sound, and one for the cable that connects to the belt pack to the actual headset. The third hole is the same as a wall jack hole, and this is where you can plug in another cable that would go to yet another headset beltpack.

If the school's budget is tight, and you can't spec as many wired wall jacks as you would like to, consider situations in which daisy-chaining would work for them, whereby you could get away with one wall jack, not two, and spec'ing more headsets. Daisy-chaining works best where the crew members don't have to move around. For instance, the Light Board Operator could daisy-chain off of the Stage Manager's beltpack if they are both sitting stationary, side by side in the booth. Although I don't thoroughly endorse it, one followspot operator could daisy-chain off of the beltpack of the other followspot operator if the followspots were next to each other. The danger of this would be having a cable strung across the catwalks or beams, which would be a tripping hazard. In addition, cues might be badly timed if one followspot operator has to relay a "Go" to the other followspot operator.

One place where daisy-chaining does not work is backstage. Crew members need to move around backstage and if one was daisy chained off even a crew member who was stationary (a Stage Manager for instance), if that mobile crew member were to walk out of cable-length range, or if someone were to trip over their cable, it could painfully yank the headsets off both of the crew members. Not only that, it could be at an inconvenient time – or potentially critical time in terms of safety – just as the Stage Manager was calling a cue or as a stationary crew member was about to execute a cue. Not to mention the cost of damaging any equipment. Plus, it could cause injury to the person tripping over the cable.

WIRED VS. WIRELESS

There are two ways headsets are powered. One way is by DC, which is batteries (rechargeables save a lot of money – you can spend hundreds of dollars a year on headset batteries - so be sure to include rechargables in your spec's or purchases). The other is by AC, which is plugged into the theatre's hardwired system by way of a cable. Both wireless and wired headsets have their benefits and you should spec some of each.

WIRED

Wired headsets don't eat up batteries, and are best for people who don't have to walk around. For instance, the light board and sound board operators don't usually have to leave their positions during a show, nor do the followspot operators, because boards and followspots are not portable. (Although, that said, even board operators occasionally have to get up from their post to attend to something that might be happening ten feet away. With a wired headset they would then would have to temporarily 'go off headset' and might miss a cue being called.)

WIRELESS

Wireless headsets are best for crew who need to move around, such as a fly system operator. They may have to fly out a drop on Lineset 6 and then rush to fly in a drop at Lineset 20. The fly rail area can be a dangerous place (see The Counterweight System chapter), and although there may be policies that any actor waiting in the wings should stay away from the fly rail, it's not always possible because of space considerations. Imagine what would happen if the crew member on a headset attached to the wall with a 20' wire were to have to move between actors and other crew standing in the wings. The cable would be a big tripping hazard.

Another person who has to move around backstage is a Mic Wrangler. This is the person who is in charge of placing mics on actors who might be sharing them, and is in charge of replacing dead batteries if they occur during a show.

Likewise for the House Manager who has to move around the lobby, in and out of audience members, concession sellers, and the box office. A cable would be very impractical.

WHO GETS WHICH

From our original list of positions, here's who should have what headset capability.

Stage Manager
　　　　The Stage Manager should have both options; a wired headset in the booth if they are calling the show from the booth and a wireless headset to wear if they are calling the show from backstage.

Light Board Operator
　　　　The Light Board operator can make do with a wired headset most of the time, but a wireless headset would be optimal.

Sound Board Operator
> The Sound Board operator (located in the house, because you've read this book) can make do with a wired headset most of the time, but a wireless headset would be optimal.

Followspot Operators
> Followspot operators rarely have to move from their positions, because they are usually located in the beams or catwalks or another position away from distractions. So they can have wired headsets. Ideally, though, they should each be able to plug into their own jacks, even if they are standing next to each other. The headset wires should be carefully located and taped down so that there is no tripping hazard.

Flyman/Fly Rail Side of the Stage
> Wireless.

Stage Right or Left – the other side of the stage from the fly rail
> Get out your crystal ball and decide if the person standing back stage will be issuing orders from where they stand, or whether they will need to move around for set changes, etc. A wired headset is better than no headset, but a wireless headset would be the best choice for flexibility in a variety of show situations.

Center of House – tech table position
> These – at least two jacks are optimal – can be wired. If someone needs to go off headset while at the tech table during a rehearsal, that's ok. It's not likely that anyone would be sitting at a tech table in the house during a show, when leaving a headset could jeopardize the show.

This all said, if you have the choice, there's almost no point in the design, labor and material costs involved in installing a wired system, as it's so restrictive. It's optimal for everyone to be able to move around with a wireless headset.

BATTERIES

And, that said, if you do go with wireless, remember to supply rechargeable batteries and chargers, because you can spend a mint on batteries if not. Be sure to purchase the chargers at the same time as you purchase the headsets. At one theatre I worked at "cost-effective" wireless headsets were purchased as a part of an upgrade, but chargers were not purchased. When I later inquired about purchasing the chargers, I was informed that the model of headset and their chargers had gone out of production. Hmm. Probably why the school district was able to get a deal? The chargers would have plugged straight into the side of the beltpack. Consequently, every time we had to replace batteries – I did at least purchase some generic chargers and rechargeable batteries – we had to open the back of the beltpack (a fiddly operation at best, which required a paper clip or penny), remove the "sled", remove the six(!) AA batteries, replace the six(!) AA batteries... Well, you get the idea – a multi part operation rather than a one part operation.

SINGLE CHANNEL VS. DOUBLE CHANNEL

One school of thought is to spec headsets with two channel capacity. The concept is so that the lighting and sound designers and their board operators can talk together in order to set the cues during tech rehearsals on one channel, and so that the set crew can all converse about the set changes on the other channel, without disrupting each other, while the Stage Manager can hear both channels because it's their job to coordinate these two groups of people and write all the cues in their prompt book or script. On the surface this seems to make sense, until reality hits and what happens is that the lighting and sound people who can't hear what the set crew are saying start talking to the SM at the same time that the set crew who can't hear that the lighting and sound people are talking start talking to the SM. Instead of being in control of the conversation and situation, the SM is hit from both sides. In addition, sometimes something the lighting and sound crew say, affect the decisions of the set crew, and visa versa. Many problems can be nipped in the bud by collaboration over the headset.

I personally prefer just to have one channel in use. If two conversations or commands need to go on at the same time, I've found that experienced crews get used to this, each person just tunes into the voice of the person that they need to be listening too. I've worked like that many a time and it works just fine if everyone cooperates.

SINGLE MUFF VS. DOUBLE MUFF

The muff is the padded ear piece that is attached to the headband that goes over the technician's head.

Always spec single muff headsets. A theatre is not a recording studio. Theatre technicians absolutely must have single muff headsets. It is essential that one ear is uncovered in order for the technicians to be able to hear what is going on around them. Technicians on stage must be aware of their surroundings. This is a huge safety issue. They must be able to hear warning calls in case a set piece falls or a pipe is coming in above their heads.

Safety aside, it is the job of all technicians to pay attention to what is going on on stage, and most importantly the Stage Manager needs to hear each line the actors say in order to call lighting, sound and set/rigging cues at the right time. Plus, an Assistant Stage Manager, Deck Manager or Stage Manager on stage must be available to answer questions from cast and crew, while also hearing what is going on at other areas of the theatre over the headset.

The sound techs need to be able to communicate with the Stage Manager and other technicians, while being able to hear what the audience hears - they cannot have false sound levels being fed into their headsets. That said, the sound technician should also have a double muff headset that is plugged into their sound board, because occasionally she needs to be able to cue up a sound effect or piece of music without the audience hearing it and without them hearing the audience.

Sometimes, when there are not enough headsets provided in a theatre, there are people who can do without. For instance, if the Stage Manager is calling the show from the booth and is sitting right next to the light board operator then there is really no need for the light board operator to have a headset, as the SM is the only person they need to receive instructions from. In this situation it's especially important not to have a double muff headset because the SM needs to have confirmation that the light board operator has received warnings, standbys and/or has completed cues. They cannot be wearing double muff headsets as they must have one ear free in order to have two way communication with the light board operator.

MUFF COMFORT

During tech rehearsals that can last around 5 to 8 hours – or longer, and during days when there are both matinee and evening performances, crew members are wearing their headsets for hours at a time. It is worth it not to scrimp on cheap headsets with uncomfortable muffs. Also keep in mind that some people have to wear eye glasses and they can have the additional discomfort of having the side of their glasses pressed against the side of their head. And, while they're removable, many people wear earrings. I myself have my favorite pair of "headset friendly" earrings (they're even black, because techies were black clothing in order not to be seen!). Regardless of what else you're wearing, I can attest to how uncomfortable, if not painful, it is to have to wear cheap headsets for hours on end.

CALL LIGHT

A call light is a little light that flashes on the beltpack when another crew member pushes their call button on their beltpack. It will flash a light on all the beltpacks, so that those not on headset know to check in.

As some point in time it may be necessary for any technician to go "off headset". Sound technicians in particular are notorious for never wearing their headsets, which bugs the heck out of the rest of the crew because they can never get a hold of them. However, there is a good reason. The sound crew need to hear what the audience hears, so they can't have their ears covered with headset muffs all the time. However, the stage manager and the rest of the technicians do have to communicate with the sound technicians at times, so make sure the headset system that you spec has a call light on the beltpack. Of course that is assuming that the sound techs have placed their beltpack in their field of vision, which is not always possible to do (say the sound board covers the entire desk surface and there is no where to put the belt pack). For this reason if at all possible, it's best to install some sort of call light at the sound board station within visual range.

CHAPTER 12

THE COUNTERWEIGHT SYSTEM

This chapter about the *Counterweight System* (or *Fly System* or *Rigging System* as it is interchangeably called) is included in this book because it's the system the stage lighting crew uses the most. Each time a light is hung a pipe it needs to be reweighted. (Unless – you spec an electric winch system for your electrics. The pros and cons of that are discussed later in this chapter.) It is also potentially the most dangerous system in the theatre, so it is included in this book because of the seriousness of the lighting crew operating this system safely.

If you're not a theatre person, the counterweight system is possibly one of the things you think about when you visualize backstage in a theatre - its' often shown in movies and TV shows. It's that row of ropes that are pulled to raise and lower scenery. But there's far more to it than just walking over to a rope and pulling on it to raise ("fly out") or lower ("fly in") a piece of scenery.

For a start, consider that you are flying hundreds of pounds of weight above the heads of people who have no hardhats on. What construction site allows that? The people below simply cannot be in the wrong place at the wrong time.

TRAINING

Anyone who will be operating the counterweight system must be taught the theory and practices of operating the system safely. Although you as an architect will not be involved in the operation of your theatre, it's important to have an understanding of the dangers of the counterweigh system, so that you can advise the administrators about its safe operation.

The operator is a part of they system. Whether a rope or cable fails or whether the operator fails, the system is compromised as a whole. The fact that as soon as someone lays hands on a rope s/he becomes a part of the system, is pause for thought. For this reason, a school must have a strict protocol about using the fly system. People should also be taught to be aware with their senses (this goes for any component system of a theatre). They should be taught to look, listen, and smell, and to report anything unusual.

Schools simply cannot send an untrained person over to the ropes and ask them to hang some lighting instruments properly from the pipes and to re-weight appropriately without any training (it's certainly not recommended that students do this, but more on that later).

As the name suggests the whole system relies on counter balancing, or "counterweighting", objects. Every time the weight hanging on a pipe is changed by adding lights, or by taking off lights, you have to "counter weight" them with something commonly called pig irons or bricks. Pig irons are iron weights that are stacked on the "arbor" which is the structure that holds them in place.

Not only does this counterweighting have to happen, but it has to happen in a specific order. It is very important to keep the majority of the weight on the stage side, so that when you load weight you load the lights first, and when you take away weight you take away from the arbor side first. Each of these procedures is designed to ensure that a heavy weight will not come crashing down onto the stage where people may be standing.

In addition, counterweight systems are generally built such that, while re-weighting, the lock can hold an imbalance of about 50lbs while re-weighting, but there are precautions you must take in order not to rely on the lock.

So serious is this procedure that there is an industry certification available for those doing stage rigging. The Entertainment Technician Certification Program certifies theatre technicians in the use of counterweight systems, and the mechanical and hydraulic systems that are usually permanently installed in theatres. To find out more go to www.etcp.plasa.org.

That said, in practice most high school theatres don't have ETCP certified riggers on staff. Even professional theatre technicians have initially learned at their own high schools, universities and/or on the job over the years. Not all high schools even hire theatre technicians, so that means that the Drama teacher has to be trained in rigging techniques and safety, but even that doesn't usually happen. And when the Drama teacher doesn't understand, or feel comfortable using, the counterweight system s/he will come to rely on students, who self-train themselves. At one high school theatre that I started working at there was a student who had taken an interest in technical theatre, and, before I came on board, he took charge of all the rigging, but had no formal procedural or safety training on running a fly system. After he graduated I actually hired him as a technician and I made sure that he went through a rigging training program through a local company.

SAFE OPERATIONS

It's not only important for a school to make sure their students go through the correct training, and have their parents sign a waiver form before they can operate the counterweight system (more on safety waivers later), but it's also very important that the school administration understands that they need to be supervised at all times and that they continue to follow the proper procedures. It's my philosophy that shows should be entirely run by students whenever possible, however there should always be a theatre technician present to supervise, even if it looks like on the surface that they aren't doing anything. As I often say, you don't send the babysitter home after the children are in bed.

RIGGING

But, how do lights get on the pipes in the first place?

Hundreds of pounds of weight is being hung above people's heads, so the proper procedures must be followed. Schools should never allow their students do this without supervision from a trained professional technician. In the process of hanging lights, safety cables must always be secured first when hanging and last when striking.

There is a proper technique and procedure for flying, and the following is a sample of a written procedure all high school theatre should have.

SAMPLE COUNTERWEIGHT SYSTEM OPERATIONS GUIDELINES

A student crew member may operate the fly system for the purposes of rehearsals and/or performances <u>after turning in the signed permission form</u> and <u>only after receiving training</u> from a theatre technician. (Only theatre technicians are authorized to lead the re-weighting of the battens.)

THE FOLLOWING PROCEDURES MUST BE FOLLOWED:
Operator must have a direct visual line to the area of the stage below the pipe (batten) that is flying in or out. If it is not possible to have a direct visual line, the operator must assign a second person to spot and relay information.

During set-up, initial rehearsals, and strikes.
Stand by the rail and look on the stage to confirm that the area is clear.
Release the safety ring around the handle and lower the handle.
Keeping both hands on the rope, turn body and head around to face stage.
Call in a LOUD voice "_____ (pipe) coming in/going out."
Wait for someone to respond "Clear" or "Thank you". This must be someone who is on stage and has actually looked to see if it is clear. If you do not hear a "Clear", call your warning again. Under

no circumstances start to lower the batten if you have not received a "Clear" even if you can see the stage yourself.

Begin to pull the rope in order to lower or raise the batten. Keep both hands on the rope at all times and continually look on the stage. If it is necessary to stop at a spike tape mark, glance occasionally at the rope, but only take your attention off the stage when close to spike.
Stop when the batten is all the way in, all the way out, or on spike. Slow down when approaching the end. Do not let the arbor crash at the stop.
Push the handle up and secure the ring around it.

During final tech rehearsals and performances.

During final tech rehearsals and performances you can't be yelling out commands. By this time performers and other crew members should know when and where scenery, drapes, etc. will be flying in and out. Therefore you do not have to call out, but, *even if you are familiar with the show by this time*, you may not move the batten until told to do so by the lead rigger or by the Stage Manager (SM) – this is called 'taking your cue'. If you have a headset, the SM will be able to talk to you directly. If not, the SM or lead rigger will signal you with a pre-determined hand movement – in this case, when your cue is coming up, you must keep your attention on whomever will be signaling you.

The SM will call, or signal, "Standby rail" or "Standby _____(batten name)".
Respond (by voice or signal) "Rail **standing by**" or "_____ standing by".
Release the ring and the handle and **place both hands on the correct side of the rope.**
IMPORTANT: DO NOT DO ANYTHING UNTIL YOU HAVE BEEN GIVEN THE "GO".
The SM will call, or signal "Go".
Unless otherwise told to do so, **pull the rope in a quick, yet controlled manner.**
Watch the stage if it is in your visual line.
Stop when the batten is all the way in/out, or on spike. Slow down when approaching the end. Do not let the arbor crash at the stop.
Push the handle up and secure the ring around it.
Respond to the SM "Rail **complete**" or "_____ complete".

Following is a sample of a basic loading policy.

SAMPLE COUNTERWEIGHT LOADING AND UNLOADING PROCEDURES

Only theatre technicians are authorized to lead the re-weighting of the battens. A student or outside event crew member may assist under the direct supervision of a theatre technician, if they have submitted a signed liability waiver form.

Counterweight loading and unloading:

TO LOAD A BATTEN SAFELY:

WITH FLYMAN AT THE LOCKING RAIL AND LOADERS ON THE LOADING GALLERY:
Flyman calls in a LOUD voice "_____ (pipe) coming in/going out" and lowers batten to the deck.
Flyman gives clearance to deck crew to place the load on batten.
AFTER load is on batten Flyman calls "Clear the stage, loading in process." All people on the stage must be at least past the center line of the stage and any doors on the working side of the stage should be locked to prevent people walking in during loading.
Flyman estimates weight and directs loaders to load the arbor with appropriate weights equal to the load.
Main loader calls "Clear the deck". The Flyman calls "Deck Clear" when everyone is on the far side of the stage and entry doors are locked.
Loaders raise keeper nuts and spreader plates, leaving one on top of batten weight. Main loader calls "Loading weights".
Loaders place required counterweights on arbor. If many "bricks" are needed, a spreader plate should be inserted between weights every two feet.
When finished, Loaders slide down remaining plates and keeper nuts, locking them in place with thumb screws. Only then do they call down: "Locked and Secured."
Flyman calls to Deck crew to "Clear the Batten."
Flyman removes keeper ring and opens lock handle, and tests load for balance. (There are procedures for securing the ropes before this step that are outside the scope of this book. Always use a trained rigging professional.)
If load is out of balance, repeat above procedure to adjust.
Once weight is correct, Flyman calls "Clear the Batten" and flies the load to trim, locking rope lock and securing with Keeper Ring.

TO UNLOAD, REVERSE THE PROCEEDURE.

WEIGHTS

It's also a good idea to provide a high school theatre a list of the weights of common instruments they will hang on the pipes, so that they don't have to weigh things or look up their weights over and over again. For instruments they do have to weigh, a good bathroom scale works fine. It's also useful for them to know the maximum weight each batten can take, although in high school theatre this is rarely exceeded. Following is a list I kept in one theatre, but please keep in mind that the weights stated are specific to the brands of instruments in that particular theatre and should only be used as estimates.

SAMPLE LIGHTING INSTRUMENT AND DROP WEIGHTS FOR COUNTERWEIGHT SYSTEM

(Please note: only theatre technicians may supervise re-weighting of pipes.)

Weight limits on battens
(Arbor lengths for each batten can be found on the theatre website under: Stage and Rigging; Linesets.)

5' arbor:	1044 lbs
6' arbor:	1300 lbs
7' arbor:	1567 lbs

Approximate weights of some lighting instruments

6" fresnel	14lbs
10" fresnel	15lbs
Ellipsoidal (not including zooms.)	19lbs
Zoom	21lbs
PARs	12lbs
3-cell LED cycs	41lbs
Single cycs	10lbs
Triple cycs	28lbs
Hid works	25lbs

LOCKOUT TAGOUT TAGS

Although a school may have trained their student crew to use the counterweight system, and although their policy may be that they may only do so under supervision of a technician, this doesn't not always happen in the high school setting. In one high school theatre that I worked at, one particular teacher would allow students to go into the theatre on their own to set up for a class or rehearsal, or he himself would sometimes fly in drapes etc. The trouble was, besides the obvious safety issues, that sometimes he or his students would grab the wrong rope and move the electrics, or the "borders" (sometimes called "teasers") which are black curtain strips that hide the production lights from the site line of the audience. The trouble with this is that the electrics and borders are set at a specific trim height, and then the lights are focused to specific areas or set pieces. Once they are focused, moving the electric that they are hung on up or down changes where they are focused. If the border is accidentally moved, it may expose the sight of the lighting instruments to the audience.

In order to prevent people from moving any lines that shouldn't be moved I recommend providing what are called "lockout tagout" tags. There are different brands and styles you can get, but I recommend ones that are specifically designed to go in the holes that fixes the rope lock handle in the locked position.

Another purpose for a lockout tagout tag is in case a line is deemed too dangerous to move for some reason, or because for some reason it has to be left temporarily out of weight (although in theory this should never happen). In this case, do not use the same lockout tagout tag that you use for your electrics and borders, because someone used to that system would not realize that in this case a real danger was present. They're not cheap, but they are a great value when you consider their purpose.

COUNTERWEIGHT SYSTEM VS. ELECTRIC WINCH SYSTEM

Most high school theatres these days have a counterweight system where the weight of the scenery or lights is counter-weighted with weights, which are moved by pulling on ropes. As you have read, if this is not done correctly this can cause a very unsafe condition. For this reason some districts are persuaded by their insurance companies to request that complete electric winch systems be spec'd instead. Electric winch systems allow the user to move the pipes with the scenery and lights on up and down with the push of a button. They winch system is strong enough to hold huge amounts of weight, thereby eliminating the need to re-weight every time you add or take off another light or piece of scenery (although the winch can be "taught" what weight it is moving). More sophisticated systems come with a computer, whereby you can program "cues". For instance, if you need to prep for a show, you enter a cue number and all of the legs and the cyc come down in place at once. If you are doing a scene change, you enter a cue number and three pieces of scenery fly out and two fly in. Presto change-o.

On the surface, this may sound far preferable in the high school theatre setting. But I haven't met a high school theatre technician yet who thinks so. There are several serious practical drawbacks to an automated winch system. They include:

> To program in, and execute, a cue needs only one person. In a high school setting where there are usually several students wanting to work backstage, this denies jobs to too many students.

> Career and Technical Educational value is lost. The high school students haven't been taught and therefore don't learn about counterweighting protocol and rigging procedures and if they go on to work in another theatre – community, college or professional, most of which have counterweight systems - they could be put themselves and others in danger with a presumed level of training that they don't have.

> Many older winch systems have a button that you must actively hold down in order for the pipe to move, however because it's so 'simple' to use, safety training is not adhered to.

> In the newer winch systems with computers there is an auto stop built into the system, so that if a drape or pipe hits an object it automatically stops moving. The trouble is, it has to hit the object first. That object could be a student's head.

> Electric winches don't know to stop when someone yells "Stop!". When a student is actively lowering a piece of scenery with a counterweighted rope system and a student on stage sees that it is *about* to hit something that was not meant to be there, the student on stage can yell "Stop!" and the student on the fly system can stop lowering the ropes in order to avoid an accident, or worse. If a student pushes a button on the computer screen of an electric winch system that student knows that the system will

do what it's programmed to do. So even if that student has been trained to stand by the screen, they are not actively doing anything, or do not appear to be doing anything to other students. If that student is distracted (say by another student – like that would happen!), when the student on stage yells "Stop!" the student operating the screen may not be able to get back to the control in time to avert the disaster.

Another perceived positive feature about an automated winch system is the ability to create "cues", where several pieces of scenery and/or drapery can fly in and/or out at the push of the button. However, consider a situation where a show is in progress and a crew member leaves a piece of scenery, say a desk, in the wrong place during the previous set change. The next set change comes along. The operator pushes the button and several pieces of scenery fly out while a some fly in. Suddenly a crew member realizes that a wall that is flying in is going to hit the desk. He yells "Stop!" over his headset to the winch operator. The winch operator quickly pushes the stop button. In a situation where a counterweight system is in use, the crew member flying in that particular wall can stop, while the remaining crew members can keep flying their set pieces and drapes. The desk is moved, and that wall continues to fly in. The audience notices nothing amiss. The show goes on. In the same scenario using an automated winch system, when the stop button is pushed all pieces of scenery stop flying in and out. The whole set change is put at a halt. This disrupts the flow of the play. A crew member manages to move the desk and the winch operator can continue the set change cue, but by this time the audience is now drawn into the situation and drawn away from the 'magic' of theatre.

Complete system failure is another risk with a winch system. One high school I'm associated with had a full winch system installed in their new theatre. Within the first two years of its operation the computer system failed several times requiring service. A well maintained counterweight system can last decades.

Even though the counterweight system may be perceived as more dangerous to an insurance agent sitting at a desk, I've never met a theatre technician who is in agreement with that perception.

Again, a student crew member actively working the ropes on a counterweight system can see a hazard about to happen – say an actor walks under a piece of scenery that is being flown in – the student crew member operating a counterweight system would see the actor moving and stop the scenery before it hit the actor on the head. A winch system would only stop itself once it sensed it had already hit something. A winch system may occasionally be more convenient, perhaps. But safer? No.

The system I like the best is a combination, where the light pipes are on a winch system and the scenery pipes are on a counterweight system. One theatre I worked in had a combination system like this and it seemed to work very well. It allows the lighting technicians and student crew to move instruments around quickly without having to close the stage in order to re-weight every single time. Also, during a show, it's very rare that a light pipe has to be brought down to the stage deck. Hanging scenery usually takes up the whole stage during the process regardless, and scenery is being moved in and out during the course of a show. So the counterweight system employs more students and, with a properly trained crew, is actually safer than a winch system.

CHAPTER 13

LIGHTING MAINTENANCE

Because a high school theatre acting as a "road house" can be very busy with school and outside events, sometimes it's all the Theatre Manager can do to just get the shows produced, and "things that should be done" get left by the wayside. Sometimes it's because these things take more time than is immediately available, sometimes it's because specialty equipment might need to be ordered, and sometimes it's because the work might take scheduling several technicians at once. There's always something that needs to be done that isn't getting done soon enough. Again, although you as an architect won't be involved in maintenance, it's good to know what the end user will be involved in, so you can design backwards in order to make their jobs easier in the long run.

WORK PARTIES

A Theatre Manager should schedule regular work "parties" (they actually can be fun!) at least twice a year - sometimes three or four times a year if need be – during the theatre's slower months. In educational theatre, I've found that good months to schedule larger maintenance projects are:

- September through early October – school events are still preparing or practicing at the start of the year, so that time is typically slow for productions.

- January through March – this is likely after your school's large fall/winter production and before your school's large spring production while rehearsals are going on.

- July and August – school is out, and many outside events take off for the summer as well.

SAMPLE SUMMER WORK PARTY TO DO LISTS

Following is one of my work party to do lists of 'saved up' jobs that we didn't have time to complete during one school year.

LIGHTING TO DO

Re-record Stage Manager Panel presets.

Re-label 1st cats non-dims and apron floods on SM Panel.

File gels.

Figure out best placement for conductor light.

Gel catwalk safety lights.

Re-gel Rep ladders. Safety cables for each work light.

Light board. Sub- pages: rep plot, rep dance plot.

Cyc lights – park LEDs to free up sub on board.

Cyc lights – switch to "smoothing"(see manual in drawer under SM Panel in booth).

Lower electrics and re-focus areas, lower borders.

Move cyc lights more center stage, move legs in.

Choir/band shell lighting. Add front lights. Focus down lights down, not as backs.

Re-gel yellow in Rep ladders.

3rd LX, fresnel plugged into circuit #114 is missing its strain relief on the cord cap.

Switch gels and channel no.s on cheat sheet for warm and cool downs

> Repatch front wash channels so that SR is SR and SL is SL
>
> Add 4th ladders to all dance subs
>
> Focus 4th ladders off cyc as needed
>
> Check saved name of rep/dance plot – re name if necessary
>
> Re-wire cables with plugs (in booth)
>
> 'Psych Cyc' Sub 17 – take out all channels but cyc
>
> Check power to gallery Edison outlets – report if not working
>
> Move LEDs to front wash position
>
> Re-patch LEDs and i-Cue to channels with faders

OFF SEASON MAINTENANCE

Summer is the best time to schedule maintenance for a school theatre. There are some items that your technicians can do (and in fact may be the only people in your district qualified to do), some items can, and should, be done by custodians who have the proper equipment, some items need to be done by your district's maintenance department, and then there are items that need to be taken care of by a professional company.

> **A FEW SUMMER MAINTENANCE TASKS FOR TECHS**
>
> Lens and reflector cleaning.
>
> Re-hang and focus rep plot.
>
> Replace burned out gels.
>
> Replace burned out lamps.
>
> Confirm lighting inventory on website.

PERPETUAL MAINTENANCE

Despite all of these maintenance to do lists, the Theatre Manager, technicians, and even the students, should pay attention to potential maintenance needs every time they are in the theatre and using the equipment. They should be aware with all of their senses. If something doesn't look, sound, smell or feel right (ok, no tasting the fly ropes) they should report it to the Theatre Manager immediately. Maintenance is the responsibility of anyone who uses a high school theatre.

CHAPTER 14

STORAGE

One common complication that plagues the light crew of a high school theatre is that of not enough storage space built into their multi-million dollar facility. Understandably space is expensive to provide and maintain, and the theatre is not the only part of a high school construction budget, however if it is the school districts plan to create a theatre program, then ample space must be provided in order for the program to function.

When storage space is planned, sets, costumes and the piano are usually taken into consideration, but not always the lighting equipment. Plus, over time, most high schools build up a large inventory that they can use or adapt for more shows down the road, so this must be taken into consideration too.

In two of the high school theatres that I worked in we stored lighting equipment in the stairwell up to the catwalks, because there was no dedicated storage space for lighting.

The items that were stored in the stairwell included:

- Instruments
- Cables
- Top hats
- Barn doors
- Safety cables

This photo shows sound cables stored on a peg board, but this can also be a good storage option for lighting cables where floor space is limited.

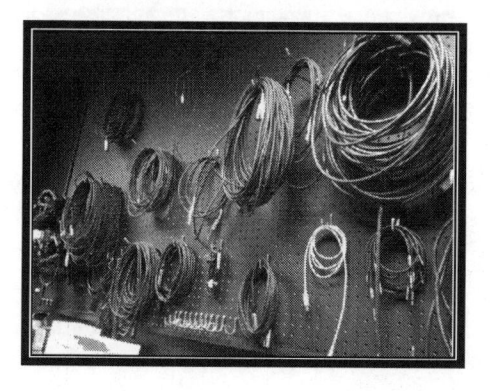

Gels are another item that need storage space. For some reason storage for gels is often an after thought.

Following are two samples of gel sheet storage. The first was made by a parent who was very adept at woodworking. The second was a map storage cabinet that was purchased.

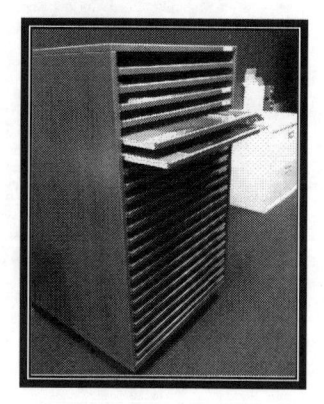

Cut gels also have to be stored. An office filing cabinet is the perfect storage space for cut gels.

A filing cabinet is also good for spare lamps, gobos and gobo holders and gel frames.

Another item that needs storage is the lenses for PAR instruments. PAR instruments are usually a common instrument spec'd in high school theatres – primarily used for ladders and down lights. Some brands of PARs provide four lenses for each instrument. Usually: a very narrow spot (15 degree beam angle), a narrow spot (19 degree beam angle), a medium flood (21 degree by 34 degree oblong beam angle), and a wide flood (30 degree by 51 degree oblong beam angle) lenses. However once hung and focused only one lens is used – often times

99

indefinitely. So space to store all the boxes with the other three lenses (one box per instrument) has to be found– just in case. If there are 24 PARs in a lighting package, you can imagine the space needed to store all the lenses in their boxes.

Cost saving is always a consideration when building a high school, but economizing on storage space while you have the capital budget to build perpetually seeps into the operations budget for the life of the school. All of the high schools I've worked at struggle with space for storage to the point that there is a lot of expensive waste. Some schools theatre departments decide to rent storage units. Some simply end up giving away or even throwing away valuable supplies and stock. In addition, a lack of storage space can cause hazardous situations, as Jo discovered in the opening vignette. The best thing to do is to visit a high school theatre that has been in operation for a decade or so, and assess their storage needs and issues.

PART 3
WHAT'S IT ALL FOR?

CHAPTER 15

STAGE LIGHTING EDUCATION

> *"So much has changed technically and yet in other ways I'm sure little has. The stuff actually happening on the stage is probably not different at all...and its got me thinking back on those years and everything I learned. Yes, about how to run a dinosaur of a light board and an arc follow spot, but really how to be part of a team and work with people and be a leader. I've learned a lot in my adult career but the things that helped me have some measure of success were the group and people skills I learned when I was 16. Plus just how to work. It's something that some people never quite learn."*
>
> - Roy Kienitz
> Former Under Secretary of Transportation,
> Obama Administration – First Term

Because a lot of new theatres are being built on school campuses, I would be remiss if I didn't address the educational benefits of stage lighting.

Obviously it is important to address education in a book about high school theatres - let's not forget the ultimate reason that a high school theatre exists – but what isn't as obvious to architects and administrators who haven't experienced the behind-the-scenes operations of their high school theatre, is the educational value. Most tech theatre students who work in your high school theatre will probably not go on to work in the entertainment industry – but then most students in a math class will probably not go on to be mathematicians – however the universal career skills and life skills they gain during their time doing technical theatre are invaluable.

In my experience over the years of working in educational technical theatre, I have found that students who work in technical theatre - from 5th graders to 12th graders - are some of the most highly motivated, dedicated, energetic, team-oriented, thick-skinned, professional-acting and technically-proficient students you can hope to work with. And if they're not, they don't last long and they quickly find that tech theatre is not for them.

When I am working with technical theatre students, I am always pleased to see that, as well as increasing their proficiency in the curriculum content, the students have further developed a broad range of skills that will benefit them throughout their lives, such as:

> creative thinking,
> teamwork,
> decision making,
> problem solving,
> perseverance,
> working with different personalities,
> working with different standards,
> analytical thinking,
> self-responsibility and
> responsibility to others.

These aren't skills you learn just by sitting in a classroom.

I am also a firm believer of providing students with as professional experience as possible. It's important to teach student crew professional protocols, and provide school groups who perform in events in your theatres with a professional experience. For that reason, the equipment you spec must be a professional grad – again, designing backwards. There is a school of thought that putting on a school show should be just for fun and it's not important to be all professional about it. I thoroughly disagree. Why are FBLA (Future Business Leaders of America) students required to dress in office attire when attending their conferences – couldn't they attend in jeans? Why do sports teams wear expensive uniforms – couldn't they play just as well in t-shirts and shorts? Why do robotics clubs, such as the renowned FIRST Robotics (www.usfirst.org), expect students to have "gracious professionalism"? For the same reasons that your events in high school theatres should be run as professionally as possible - to teach students the professional standards, equipment and systems that they will encounter in the 'real world'.

REAL WORLD APPLICATIONS

Only a small percentage of the students in a high school tech theatre program will actually go on to make some aspect of technical theatre their career, just as in any given subject in high school, but the skills all students learn in tech theatre are transferable to a wide variety of jobs. I have a favorite quote that I always hang on the tech booth wall of any theatre that I work in and it reads:

"An actor without techies is a naked person standing in the dark trying to emote.
A techie without actors is a person with marketable skills."

High school technical theatre students who do go on to work in the Entertainment Industry are not just "skilled labor" but leaders, innovators and collaborators. Designers, managers and technicians in the Entertainment industry are the backbone of every event our society. We often think of them in live theatre, sitcoms and movies, but they also work for:

political rallies,
sporting events,
concerts,
documentaries,
radio programs,
Olympic games,
amusement parks,
conferences,
tradeshows,
press conferences,
circuses,
museums…

For students who may not go on to pursue a degree or career in the entertainment industry, the transferable skills and knowledge learned in technical theatre are relevant to a wide variety of careers that have similar knowledge bases and practices as technical theatre such as:

architecture,
construction,
engineering,
science,
people management,
project management,
art,
technology,
computer drafting and design,
computer programming,
robotics…

Here are some related areas of interest that my tech theatre students have been interested in or have gone on to work in:

physics,
photography,
engineering,
construction,
computer programming,

CAD,
art,
graphic design,
website design.

Those that have chosen to work in the theatre industry have got themselves jobs as

professional lighting technicians,
technical directors,
lighting designers,
stage managers,
theatre teachers
and more.

IN DEMAND JOB SKILLS

Working on a stage crew helps prepare students with 8 of the most In-Demand Job Skills in today's world. The following list is from an article on the Monster website, by James C. Gonyea, which lists skills that the US Department of Labor says are on employers' wish lists. The underlined words indicate a job skill that is used when working on a stage crew.

Problem-Solving Skills

"Many of the tasks we face each day in our personal and business lives are complex in nature. People who can identify problems, research solutions and make effective decisions are increasingly desired in such fields as business administration, management consulting, public administration, science, medicine and engineering."

If you ever have the opportunity, sit in on a Production Meeting between student set crew members and their set designer. It is the embodiment of problem solving. The director wants this and that for their set and the designer and crew have to figure out how to build the set within budget, within time, within ease of set changes, with a restriction on space in the scene shop and back stage, within safety requirements and within the director's vision of how the play should look. This is one big problem solving festival!

Vocational-Technical Skills

"Today, technology is advanced in all areas of human endeavor. Installation, testing and repair of most electrical, electronic and mechanical equipment in fields such as engineering, telecommunications, automotive, transportation and aerospace requires people with advanced vocational-technical skills."

These skills are practiced in the theatre time and time again. Plays are temporary things. The set design and the lighting and sound has to be installed, tested, repaired, taken down, and done all over again for the next play. Students receive continuous hands-on experience.

Human Relations Skills

"All companies with more than one employee face inevitable problems dealing with how people interact with each other. Often, <u>the success of a company depends upon how well people can work together</u>. It is the job of human resource managers, personnel officers, department managers and administrators to understand the needs of workers and how best to meet those needs within the confines of the employment environment."

Human relations skills are inherent in the theatre. There are so many specialties, each with their own knowledge and temperaments, and they all have to work together to create an end product. If they can't work well together then the end result – the play – wouldn't happen.

Computer Programming Skills

"Understanding <u>how to harness a computer's power and program it to meet the specific needs</u> of a particular company can dramatically increase your employment opportunities. Specific languages most in demand today include C++, Java, HTML, Visual Basic, Unix and SQL Server."

Set builders and lighting technicians use CAD (Computer Aided Drafting). Lighting technicians and sound technicians have computer boards they have to 'harness' and program for each show.

Teaching-Training Skill

"Our modern society develops and collects more new data in a day than our ancestors did in a year. As a result, there will continue to be a demand for <u>people with teaching and training skills</u> in the fields of education, social services, management consulting and commerce."

Students may not go on to be teachers, but in the business world training happens all the time. It can be a formal training session, or integrated on the job training. Students only stay in a high school for four years. Those with more experience in technical theatre take new students under their wing and teach them the trade. Those students then 'raise up the ranks' and in turn teach the next lot of students. Teaching skills develop organically in tech theatre.

106

Science and Math Skills

"Great advances are being made daily in the fields of science, medicine and engineering. <u>Bright minds skilled in the sciences and math</u> are needed to meet the challenges of these fields."

Bright minds indeed. Try figuring out the dimensions of set pieces, how long to cut a board of wood for a set or a piece of material for a costume, the angles of light, the physical properties of light and sound – where is science and math not used in some form in technical theatre.

Information Management Skills

"In the Age of Information, America now produces information as the basis of its economic system, and <u>individuals who possess the ability to manage information</u> are critical to most businesses. Systems analysts, information technologists, database administrators and telecommunication engineers are examples of people with highly developed information management skills."

Information management is also inherent in the tech theatre setting. Students must manage information, analyze systems, and create databases just in order to create sets, lights, sound and costumes. You can't do your job in the theatre without information management.

Business Management Skills

"The business of America is business! Understanding of how to run a successful company is highly in demand. At the core of these skills is <u>the ability to manage people, systems, resources</u> and finances; to understand the needs of consumers and how to translate those needs into business opportunities."

A play is essentially a company, with people, systems, resources and finances that are working towards creating a business opportunity – the play – in order to fulfill the needs of their consumers – the audience. It's not called Show *Business* for nothing.

STTEM

What a lot of people also don't realize is that Tech Theatre is a STEM subject – or as I prefer a STTEM subject. Most people think only of the performing "arts" when they think of a high school theatre. In actuality, tech theatre is...

where

Science
Technology
Teamwork
Engineering
Mathematics

support the Arts.

"As a CEO of a science center – one of my goals is to expose kids to the idea of careers that use STEM education – i.e. stage designers and technicians being one of them. Using theatrical tech as a way of teaching science and engineering is a good way for us to get to the kids."

- Phil Lindsey
CEO Mobius Children's Museum & Mobius Science Center, Spokane, WA

LEARNING GOALS

Participation on a technical theatre crew incorporates many of the learning goals that states require in order for students to be prepared for the in-demand job skills in today's STTEM-oriented work world. Following is a study I once did on the Learning Goals for students on a stage lighting crew.

Students on the Stage Lighting Crew will learn how to:

think creatively
use technology
work as a team
make decisions
be responsible
problem solve
think analytically
be leaders

Stage lighting is a discipline that utilizes a blend of artistry, technical knowledge, physical effort and life skills. Lighting is a very specialized field which incorporates a broad range of skills such as: creative thinking, use of technology, use of mathematics, team work, decision making, problem solving, perseverance, working with different personalities and standards, analytical thinking, and responsibility.

The learning objective is that students will be able to demonstrate artistic design theory and techniques such as color theory, use the four properties of light for mood manipulation and perform drafting basics, and demonstrate the above range of skills. Not only will students gain knowledge about a unique subject, but the skills students learn and use while working on a lighting crew will benefit them throughout their lives.

GOAL: reading, comprehension, communication

Students must be able to read and quickly comprehend scripts, instructions, cue sheets and technical data. They must be able to clearly and effectively, through written and verbal means, communicate to other members of the production team, through the use of cue sheets, script cues and other written information pertinent to the production.

GOAL: mathematics, science, arts, fitness

Stage Lighting utilizes a blend of technical knowledge, artistry and physical effort.

Students will apply the concepts and principals of math and science in their work. They must be able to do basic algebra and will apply this computational knowledge to the study of electricity. Light itself is a radiant energy in one octave of the electromagnetic spectrum, identified by frequency of wavelength. The color of light is a fascinating scientific phenomenon to study in and of itself. The use of technology is also incorporated into Stage Lighting, as students learn how to use a light board. Students also have to opportunity to take apart lighting instruments, to see how they are designed, how they work and for what applications they are used. Historically lighting was an engineering discipline, and it is only in recent decades that those with a knowledge of the science of lighting have combined it with their artistic talents to become Lighting Designers.

To some extent artistry may be an inborn trait, however art techniques can be taught, and the artistic talent, which I believe is within each of us, can be tapped. The students will learn about color choices, mixing colors, how different light angles affect the viewer's perception of an object, how to enhance an "object" (usually an actor or set piece), and how to create mood using color, angles and intensity of light. These disciplines draw from both scientific fact and artistic talent. Drafting is also an important skill that Lighting Designers must know in order to communicate their design (the Light Plot) to the crew. Being able to draft and read a Light Plot is essential. Student will learn some basics about drafting for Stage Lighting.

Once the lighting plot is drafted, little time is spent sitting at a desk. Hanging and Focusing a production can be quite a rigorous task; ladders to climb, heavy instruments to carry, bolts that won't loosen, a lot of walking around and running here and there! At Bear Creek Elementary, because of liability issues, the children are not permitted to go up on our Genie Lift to hang and focus lights (yours truly will do that!). However, I encourage children to come and help out at a Hang and Focus session, so that they can be a part of the process.

GOAL: think analytically, thinking creatively, problem solving

Analytical thinking, problem solving, and creativity are very important in stagecraft, as every play, show, dance and assembly is different. Students need to draw from what they have learned to integrate their experience and knowledge and apply it to each production. Each design will be different, and the problems that come up will be different for each production. Through their participation in workshop classes, shows and assemblies this year, the students will learn theory and practical lessons, and apply it to their own design at the end of the year.

GOAL: relate school experiences and learning to career

While not everyone will pursue being a Stage Lighting Designer as a career (and there are those who manage to make a living from it), the skills learned from one's experiences in the educational setting can help prepare students for the "outside world". These skills include, but are not limited to: responsibility, dependability, attention focusing, teamwork and problem solving.

In technical theatre (including the educational experience), as in many job situations, you are often the only person who can do your job. You turn up through sickness and in health. While lead actors will often have understudies, this is not the case with the tech crew. If you don't turn up one day it may be quite difficult for someone not familiar with what you were doing to take over. When you are the Light Board Operator, for instance, your job can be quite complicated. It is the Light Board Operator's responsibility to the Lighting Designer to know how to run the board, make accurate records at rehearsals, so that the cues can be duplicated, as designed, at the next rehearsal and at performances. It is also the Light Board Operator's responsibility to the cast to write down cues and notes clearly so that someone could take over in an emergency. The Lighting Designer and his or her crew have a responsibility to the director and the cast to execute appropriate cues at the correct time, with the correct emphasis.

Rehearsals can sometimes be long and tedious. Students must be able to focus their attention for an extended period of time. Rehearsals can also be hectic and frustrating at times. Students must also be able to focus their attention in this sort of environment on the instructions given to them, and to quickly and correctly record and execute the cues each time.

Teamwork involves people of different skills and backgrounds working together to create one end result, in this case, a show. Working on a team can be challenging, because while people with different skills and mind sets are needed to fill each discipline it can also be hard to work with someone who doesn't think quite like you do. The teamwork we experience in the Lighting Crew helps students learn to work with different people, to appreciate these differences, to see how they can be valuable. The students learn how to work as a leader one minute and a follower the next. For example, Lighting Designers are experts at what they do. They are in charge of the crew who is running the show, and have the responsibility of creating the best lighting design, with the artistic and technical knowledge they have acquired. Yet, ultimately, the director is in charge, so the designer must use their skills to make the director's vision come to life. The Lighting Designer simultaneously leads the light crew, and is lead by the director. Teamwork is often like this in the "real" work world. You may be a leader in your field, but at the same time, you can be a subordinate to a "boss" or other company. Learning how to combine these two begins at school, and probably takes a lifetime to master.

IN THE EDUCATIONAL SETTING

What do these goals look like in the real life educational setting?

The learning process for technical theory would start with students demonstrating an understanding of "easy electricity" for stage lighting, by role playing a human model of an electrical circuit. Students will also be able to state electrical calculations (integrating skills and concepts from other disciplines) needed specifically for the application of stage lighting. The learning objective for artistic theory would include students being able to demonstrate the McCandless Method of Lighting the Stage and the four properties of light as applicable to design. Students would demonstrate a working knowledge of color theory, mood and lighting motivation, with a hands-on session on color manipulation and design. This section would incorporate art and design concepts children may already have a previous knowledge of. Students will also be able to define the historical periods of stage lighting (recognizing the arts from a variety of historical periods, and understanding the role of the arts in the historical development of cultures).

The learning process by the end of practical application sessions would include students being able to demonstrate how their school's lighting system works, how to draft a light plot using templates and correct drafting techniques (connecting the concepts and skills from one art form to another), how to run the light board and house lights, and how to hang and focus lights for a physical, hands on understanding of stage lighting artistry and technology (if applicable – some schools do not allow the children to do this, in that case they would have the opportunity to observe a hang and focus session). Students would also have the opportunity to take apart the various light fixtures at their school, and would be able to relate how they are designed and how they work to the design applications they are used for. By the end of the workshop students will also be able to demonstrate how to write and read cues, how to Stage Manage a show and how to call the cues. In addition, throughout the year students could also take it in turns to be supervised in running the light board and stage managing any productions and/or assemblies that the school would put on (demonstrating and responding to proper etiquette in art settings and performances, and applying a performance process in the arts).

Students can create a lighting design of their own (develop, organize, apply and refine a creative process with instructor direction, assistance and independently, also selecting, developing, rehearsing and presenting refined work using a performance process, and evaluating art presentations of self), thus demonstrating that the learning objectives had been met. This could take the form of a composition designed to a piece of music with manikins or models to stand in as dancers, or coincide with a school production such as an assembly, dance workshop, variety show or play (personal feelings and ideas through a variety of forms, using the arts for inspiration and persuasion, and identify how criteria impacts personal decision making).

A field trip could be arranged to a local community theatre, for a tour of their stage and lighting system. This could be timed to coincide with a dress rehearsal, so that the students also have the opportunity to observe and critic someone else's design process and outcome. The learning objective is that students will attempt to analyze evaluate and interpret works of drama using concepts and vocabulary, and analyze theatre and visual arts encountered in daily life.

Additional sessions with the students could address architectural lighting specialties. This would give students an opportunity to relate how an interest in lighting design can be turned into a lucrative career outside of the theatre. Students will also be informed of where to go for further education in this field (connections between the arts and other disciplines, understanding and applying the role of art in the world of work.)

Lighting can also be integrated into curricula in many ways. In an art class students can be taught to see how painters, photographers and other artists use light in their work. In a technical drafting class teachers can incorporate drafting lighting plots for the stage and or lighting plans for buildings. When studying architecture teachers could incorporate architectural lighting as a part of their lesson plans. The history of lighting is quite fascinating and could be incorporated into history or social sciences lessons about how people once lived. Electrical theory will fit in well within a science curriculum. Figuring out lighting needs for the theatre primarily uses the formula W=VA (watts equals volts times amps), which is an exercise in simple algebra and can be incorporated into classroom math problems. Stage lighting is a discipline that draws from many aspects of the standard curriculum.

CTE – VOCATIONAL EDUCATION

The same fulfillment of learning goals would be applicable to any discipline in technical theatre. But who is going to create this tech class if the drama teacher doesn't know the technical side of the craft? In previous schools I've been in sometimes the drama teacher does teach the tech class, in other schools I've seen the speech and debate teacher, and an English teacher, and even the auto shop teacher, have an affinity for technical theatre – set building in particular. Sometimes a teacher knows one aspect (lights, sound, sets, costumes) of technical theatre and has guest professionals come in to teach other specialties. Sometimes I've had product reps come in for free.

Rarely have I seen a dedicated tech theatre teacher teach tech theatre in high schools, despite the fact that most states have some sort of career and technical education (CTE) requirements, which encompass subjects in highly-skilled, high demand careers, such as auto shop, culinary, media, health industry, information technology, and so on, the primary purpose of which is to provide career and technical education training and employment preparation. These courses connect classroom learning directly to the 'real world', and also offer students opportunities for job shadowing, internships as well as field trips and guest speakers coming into the classroom. And the "three R's" are integrated into the curriculum. Teachers of these programs are highly qualified, and must have had a certain amount of hours (in terms of years) of paid work in the field they are teaching.

Again, rarely have I seen technical theatre given the attention that woodshop, auto shop, culinary arts and fashion design are given in high schools, despite the fact that the Department of Labor and Industries prohibits children under 18 to be engaged in occupational activities, such as working with power tools, hoisting heavy objects and working at heights, except for those enrolled in an educational program with a vocationally certified instructor. Some states even have a Tech Theatre CTE program available, yet not all districts incorporate Tech Theatre into their curriculums, despite having multi-million dollar performing arts facilities on their high school campuses.

Your state may have a similar program. But even if it does not, the point is that only someone with a technical theatre background should be teaching technical theatre – they should be "Highly Qualified", just as math, art and sports teachers are required to be "Highly Qualified". That sentence sounds like a no-brainer, but I've seen so many schools where this is not the case. And not only that, I've seen students who have self-taught themselves more than the teacher knows in some schools. It's not only a huge liability in terms of student safety, but it's an educational disgrace.

In a CTE Tech Theatre class students learn design concepts, use of technology, problem solving and analytical thinking. They also develop self-confidence, leadership skills, creative thinking, teamwork, decision making, and responsibility to self and others – the 'lessons' that cannot be learned from a book. In addition, because not all students will go on to work for Cirque du Soleil or design the Super Bowl Half Time Show, students benefit from a myriad of transferable life skills and competencies that will put them in good stead in many industries.

The objectives of this type of program are as follows:

- Students will demonstrate specific subject knowledge about design concepts, use of technology, problem solving and analytical thinking by following the procedures for running a production.
- Student will demonstrate self-confidence, leadership skills, creative thinking, teamwork, decision making, and responsibility to self and others by their actions in the context of a show setting.
- Students will demonstrate the attainment of transferable life skills and competencies, regardless of whether they pursue a future in the entertainment industry, by documenting these in a variety of college and career applications.
- Students who otherwise are not succeeding in school will demonstrate a sense of value and inspiration to succeed by working with dedication in the theatre discipline.

An educational situation without instructional strategies is akin to students in an art classroom without a teacher present – they can figure out how to paint a picture or make a sculpture, but they haven't been taught relevance; theory, techniques, tool usage, etc. This applies to the three main aspects of technical theatre; lighting, sound and rigging. In lighting for instance, left to their own devices students can turn on the board and bring the lights up and down, they can even figure out how to record and execute cues. However, they don't know McCandless theory, they don't know dance lighting techniques, they don't know how to analyze a script or show running order, they don't know how to apply the 4 properties of light, they don't know how to patch a light board, they don't know color theory, they don't know cuing techniques, etc.

Without a CTE class in existence the system in a lot of schools limits the number of students who may participate in technical theatre and limits diversity. Here's how this happens: when a student auditions for a show, they are typically asked on the audition form if they want to do tech if they are not cast, therefore the tech crew is mostly, and sometimes only, made up of students who have a primary interest in acting. The tech crew is also limited to those students (along with their parents – for transportation in some cases) who are available after school hours. Although the tech crew is presumably open to every student in the school, non-theatre students do not have a sense of what is involved, so they don't sign up. It's the students who have an aptitude towards wood work, metal work, math, art, film studies, science and engineering, computer programming, etc. who would benefit the most from technical theatre, yet they aren't encouraged to participate.

With a CTE program, a system is also in place in order to determine benchmarks and to measure expected outcomes of the program, which are different for each specialty (lights, sound, rigging), and to assess each student's knowledge base.

These assessments will be primarily formative, because of the "on the job training" nature of the work. For example, the teacher requires the student to set-up/run equipment, the teacher asks guiding questions, then the teacher modifies the student's level of involvement in activities based on feedback in terms of performance reflecting knowledge base and ability.

However, summative assessments can also be used. These can be in the form of written reflections and/or questionnaires (written assessment), mock show compositions and models (kinetic assessment), periodic assessment meetings (verbal assessment), etc. Written CTE tests assess recalled knowledge; the correct use of vocabulary, nomenclature, procedures, appropriate equipment usages, etc. For instance, my son comes home at the start of every year with tests about every piece of machinery and power tool in the woodshop at his school and has to pass those written tests with a 100% score and demonstrate a prescribed level of competence before being permitted to use any given piece of machinery or power tool. Such is not the case without a Technical Theatre CTE program in place.

Following is Washington State's CTE Program Standards for Stage Lighting, under the Theatre Design Technology section:

10: Lighting Principles, Design Specifications and Duties of a Light Board Operator/Follow Spot Operator
    10.01-Describe the optics of lighting instruments
    10.02-Identify the purpose and usage of the ellipsoidal spotlight
    10.03-Identify the purpose and usage of the fresnel spotlight
    10.04-Identify the purpose and usage of the strip/cyc lighting instruments
    10.05-Identify and operate the follow spot
    10.06-Read and interpret a standard light plot
    10.07-Interpret a standard instrument schedule
    10.08-Identify appropriate stage lighting equipment
    10.09-Hang and circuit lights for a stage production
    10.10-Focus lights for a stage production
    10.11-Program and execute cues on a computerized lighting console
    10.12-Execute cues using a follow spot

PROFESSIONAL TECHNICIANS AS MENTORS

Many school districts think they cannot afford to hire professional technicians to staff their theatres, but consider this – technicians are generally paid even less than teachers. The technicians are "guest teachers" – at much lower cost than the hourly rate of a teacher. The technicians have the education and real world knowledge of the subject that they can impart to the students. An educational situation without instructional strategies is akin to students in a wood shop or metal shop class or an art classroom without a teacher present – they can figure out how to paint a picture or make a sculpture, they could figure out how to use the equipment and come up with ideas of things to build and create, but they haven't been taught theory, techniques, tool usage, etc. In the theatre students inherently learn while "on the job", and programs can be set up that will maximize student learning; providing real-world experience and transferable personal and career skills for all performing students, and vocational training for tech theatre students.

Technicians work in the capacity of mentors for the student crews. This can often mean a lot of sitting around appearing to do nothing, so much so that non-theatre people wonder why they are paying the technicians and not just letting the students run the shows as they seem so capable. What non-theatre people don't understand is the 'hurry up and wait' nature of the theatre. There can be lulls in the action – the lighting people sit around waiting for a sound problem to be resolved, the sound people sit around waiting for a set moving issue to be rehearsed, everyone sits around waiting to take their cues at the right time, and so on. But the technicians need to oversee the students at all times, watching for "teachable moments", because by running tech themselves without a mentor the students do not learn the curriculum of the subject. At the very least, students should be supervised by one lighting technician, one sound technician and one rigging/backstage technician. Technicians in each area not only provide safety, but they also provide the students with a real world education that will serve the students with life skills no matter what profession they end up in.

TECH THEATRE AND ACADEMIC SUCCESS

Technical theatre also benefits those students who are not succeeding "academically", who need to find a reason, and passion, to stay in school. They discover a sense of value and gain the inspiration to succeed in school in general by working with dedication in the theatre discipline. A theatre education research study, cited in the Alliance for Theatre and Education's website states that students involved in theatre production outscored non-arts students in standardized testing and that there was a measurable correlation between involvement in the theatre and academic achievement. In addition, theatre helps to improve school attendance and reduce high school drop out rates. Not only that, but involvement in the theatre builds social and communication skills, and improves self-concept and confidence.

I have seen this first hand more times than I can count where technical theatre benefits those students who are not succeeding "academically", who need to find a reason, and passion, to stay in school. I once had a fifth grade student who was a wiz on the light board – you only had to give him half an instruction and he was off – yet I later discovered he could barely write a full sentence. I've seen high school students who come from unfortunate family situations who find personal power in tech theatre. I've seen students who were only scraping by in math, science and English totally understand how to design and build a set and communicate the process to others. One student at a school where I worked was barely scraping by in high school. He eventually graduated and in a local newspaper article was quoted as saying that the only thing that had made him want to come to school everyday and do his course work was his involvement in the Drama department. Without that, he would have left school. The list goes on and on. This isn't just regarding students today, this is a timeless problem. Even in my own high school there were students who were not doing well in school and excelled in technical theatre. For instance, one such high school classmate of mine is now a technician for Cirque du Soleil.

FINALE

CHAPTER 16

BLACKOUT

I was once working in a high school theatre when the principal came through with a group of people in tow. I later discovered that this was the administration and architects from another school that was building a theatre. The principal proudly showed them around the impressive-looking state-of-the-art theatre facility, but what he didn't know about were the functional problems that existed behind the façade.

In that particular theatre the issues ranged from a tech booth counter that was too low, such that when the light board operator and Stage Manager sat down they couldn't see the stage, to a scene shop that had been placed alongside the back wall of the stage with no hallway in between, such that it was the only entrance to upstage right (think: little girls in ballet shoes entering the stage through a nail and screw ridden scene shop). Another major functional issue with that particular high school theatre was that in order to save money at the time of building there was no access to the stage right galleries – where lights are hung, and directors are fond of putting actors. If you were up in the galleries focusing lights and you discovered you needed a gel frame, you would have to walk up to the catwalks, across the catwalks, down three stories of the stairs behind the stage left galleries, through the house, up to the booth, get the gel frame, walk back down through the house, up the three stories of stage left gallery stairs, across the catwalks and back down the stage right galleries. A simple ladder under the stage right galleries would have sufficed and not broken the budget. It would have been much more helpful to the visitors to be able to sit down with my theatre staff and the tech theatre students that I worked with in order to help them avoid many function pitfalls such as these. But it was simply because the principal had never worked 'in the trenches' of the theatre in his building that he was unaware of these issues and wouldn't have known to mention them to his visitors.

As you can see it's so important for you the architect to understand high school theatre operations in general and the stage lighting system specifically, and to have the conversation not only with the administration but also with the actual users, about how the school's theatre will be operated (and funded!) in the long run, because this vision will determine the design decisions made now.

If you are designing a high school theatre's lighting system I strongly encourage you to sit down with the technical staff of local high school theatres. Plus, don't discount tech theatre students. I can't count the amount of times I've heard a tech theatre student exclaim "what were they thinking?!" It's simply the cry of a person who has to work in a space designed and managed by people who, through no fault of their own, don't have the experience of being 'in the trenches'.

If this book has thoroughly overwhelmed you by now, and you've come to realize that there is much more to designing a lighting system and running a high school theatre than my administrator and his guests did, then I've done my job. I hope this book has helped you, at least virtually, experience the trenches of technical theater, and given you a more in depth look at the requirements of high school theatre lighting systems.

It's my passion to help architects to be able to understand the behind the scenes operations that they normally wouldn't have a chance to see. If you don't have access to a theatre professional who can facilitate a collaborative dialog that will reveal approaches where high school theatre lighting system design can alleviate unexpected operational costs of educational theatre operation, then I hope this book has given you an advantageous peek into the world of high school theatres.

High school theatre managers and lighting technicians can only accomplish their mission with your help. If the lighting system is appropriately designed, then the students will be the stars!

Break a leg!

GLOSSARY OF THEATRE TERMS

* indicates that the definition of this term can be found in the Glossary.

Spelling: you will see hyphens and spaces and compound words used interchangeably. For example: off-stage, off stage, offstage or stage-right, stage right or stageright.

APRON
The part of the stage deck* that is downstage* of the proscenium*.

APRON STRIP LIGHTS
This is a band of lights – usually blue - that goes from one side of the stage to the other, just upstage of the stage deck that covers the pit, so that when the pit is open they warn a performer (who can be blinded by the production lights shining in their eyes) where the edge of the stage is. Some apron strip lights have a small red light in the middle, which dancers can use for spotting, and to let all performers know where the center stage line is.

ARBOR
The framework that holds the pig irons* that counter balance the weight of anything hung on the battens* in the counterweight system*.

ARM
The strip of stage deck* that protrudes out along the wall of the house* alongside the front part of the seating.

BACKSTAGE
The area of the stage deck* that is hidden from the audience's view, either by drapes* or set pieces.

BATTENS or PIPES
The pipes that hang above the stage and hold lights, mics and scenery. The pipes that hold the lights are called Electrics* and the pipes available for scenery hanging are called GPs*. Another common pipe is the Cloud Truss*.

BEAMS or CATWALKS
The beams or catwalks are the area above the house* where lighting instruments are hung, and sometimes followspots* are located. The term "beam" actually refers to a closed space built above the ceiling of the house, while the term "catwalk" actually refers to a metal walkway structure that hangs below the ceiling of the house. However, in the industry, the terms are loosely interchanged.

BLACK BOX
Short for "Black Box Theatre", which is a small theatre that is usually just one large, windowless room. The walls are painted black and the drapes are black, hence the name. The audience is usually set up on risers, which allows for different configurations for the stage space – proscenium*, thrust* or theatre-in-the-round. The backstage space is created with drapes or flats*.

BLACK MASKING
When the "Black Masking" is referred to it is specifically indicating the black masking* that hangs upstage and covers the length of the stage. It usually hangs just in front of or just behind the cyc*.

BLACKOUT
This is the term for when all of the stage lights are turned out at one time. It usually depicts the end of a scene or a dance.

BLACKS
Technicians* working backstage must wear dark or black clothing, so that if they happen to move within sight of the audience they will be less noticeable than a flash of white or light color clothing. The general term for their dark clothing is "blacks", as in "Don't forget to wear your blacks, it's opening night."

BLOCKING
Blocking is the term for where the actors move. Setting the blocking is like choreographing a dance. Actors have to learn their blocking as well as their lines.

BOOMS or BOX BOOMS
This is a lighting position, typically recessed into the side walls of the house* near the stage, which typically run vertical. The booms can either be accessed from the front from a ladder set in the house, or from behind via a walkway.

BOOTH
The term "Booth", when used alone, refers to the small room at the back of the House* where some of the Technicians* sit during a rehearsal or show. It usually consists of a light board, sometimes the Followspot * can be in there, a projector, and a place for the Stage Manager* to sit. The sound board is typically (or should be!) in the House*. Not to be confused with the term Ticket Booth*.

CABLE
A cable is a conduit that houses sound or lighting wiring. In the theatre they are almost always black. They are not, as in the 'outside world', referred to as "extension cords".

CAST
A collective term for the people who are performing – it may be a play or a ballet. Musicians are usually referred to as "performers", however in general the cast refers to the group of performers you see on the stage, as opposed to the crew* who work backstage and run equipment, who you don't see.

CATWALKS or BEAMS
The catwalks or beams are the area above the house* where lighting instruments are hung, and sometimes followspots* are located. The term "beam" actually refers to a closed space built above the ceiling of the house, while the term "catwalk" actually refers to a metal walkway structure that hangs below the ceiling of the house. However, in the industry, the terms are sometimes loosely interchanged. The catwalks are also referred to as the "cats".

CLEAR!
A word called out when someone on stage is responding to a warning that a pipe* or batten* is about to fly in or out. Clear should not be called until the person on stage has ascertained that the area is actually clear.

CLOUDS
Clouds are hard shells that are usually permanently hung from a batten*. They hang vertically, but once flown in to the appropriate height they open up to hang horizontally. They create a "ceiling" above a band or orchestra that bounces the sound into the audience. Some clouds have lights installed in them and some hang between light battens*, in both cases to provide down light for musicians to see their music.

CLOUD TRUSS
This is the batten* on which the clouds* are hung. This batten is different in that it usually consists of three pipes* hung in a triangular formation, which can better carry the heavy weight of the clouds*.

CONCESSIONS
This term refers to the food and drinks that are sold at a performance, typically during intermission, however some places sell concessions before and after a performance as well.

COSTUME SHOP
This is the room backstage where the costumes are created, sewn, fitted and stored.

COUNTERWEIGHT SYSTEM or FLY SYSTEM or RIGGING
This is the system of ropes that you typically see back stage in a theatre. The term "counterweight" comes from the fact that the scenery* or lighting instruments* are in some way counter weighted so that the weights on one end of the ropes weigh as much as the scenery* or lighting instruments* on the pipes, so that they are easy for one person to move in and out. These days it's most common to find pig irons* providing the counterweights, however some theatres still use sand bags. Some

rigging systems use winches, which can adjust to the weight of the scenery* or lighting instruments*, and do not require physical re-weighting by technicians*.

CREW
A collective term for the people who work backstage and run the equipment needed for a show. In order to avoid confusion, in a high school, the crew usually refers to the students, while the technicians* usually refers to the district employees that staff the theatres.

CUE
This is the term for the action a technician* takes when executing their job and usually denotes a change of some sort. For instance: a lighting cue can be a change in the lighting "look" or intensity; a sound cue can be a change in volume; a set cue can be where the set crew moves out one or more set pieces and moves in one or more others.

CYC
The cyc is the large piece of white (or off-white) material that is hung towards the back of the stage (upstage*). The full term is "cyclorama", and it is so named because the single piece of material used to circle the sides and back of the stage – you still sometimes see this in film. The cyc costs as much as a car. This is because it is one seamless piece of material that can have dimensions as long as 40' or more. As of this writing, there are only 3 places in the world that manufacture cycs. The cyc is used to project colored and/or patterned lights on, in order to create mood, or to depict time of day, or location. Such as a dark blue cyc is a sky at night, a green cyc might depict a forest. An amber cyc might be used for an up-beat jazzy piece of music and a lavender cyc might be used for a mellow jazz piece.

DECK
This is the common term for the floor surface of the stage.

DOWNSTAGE
Most people have no trouble remembering stage left* and stage right* as being from the actor's perspective, however remembering which is upstage* and downstage is harder. Downstage is towards the audience and upstage is towards the back wall of the stage. Here's how to remember: These days our stages are usually, mostly level, while the house* is raked*. In Shakespearean times the floor where the audience stood or sat was level, while the stage was raked. So when the actors walked towards the audience, they were literally walking down hill (down the stage) and when the actors walked away from the audience, towards the back wall of the stage, they were literally walking up hill (up the stage). Hence the terms upstage and downstage.

DRAPES
Short for draperies. Sometimes called the "soft goods*". This usually refers to any permanently hung pieces of material, such as the legs*, the mid-traveler*, the masking* and the cyc*.

DRESS REHEARSAL
This is the final rehearsal (or sometimes two) before opening night. The actors are in full costume and make-up and know all their lines and blocking*, the technicians* and/or crew* wear their blacks* and know all their cues*. The dress rehearsal is traditionally run without stopping in order to simulate a real performance. If someone makes a mistake it is dealt with as if an audience were watching.

DROP
A drop or "backdrop" is a painted piece of material that is hung across the stage. It usually depicts a location of the whole play or of a specific scene.

EDISON or STAGE PIN or THREE PRONG TWIST
These are the there most common types of lighting instrument* plugs and outlets that you will find in the theatre. Edison refers to your standard household plug. Stage pin also has three pins or prongs, but they are in alignment. Three prong twist has three pins or prongs that form a circle, one prong has a tab and once the plug is inserted into the outlet it is twisted to secure it.

ELECTRIC
The electric is a term that collectively refers to the pipe* on which the lighting instruments* are hung along with the raceway* into which the lighting instruments* are plugged.

FLAT
This refers to the wall of a set*. It is made of a wooden framework in the back, and is either covered with muslin (a "Broadway flat") or luaun plywood (a "Hollywood flat").

FLOOR POCKET
This is a square hole in a stage deck* that is covered with a trap door. The floor pockets can be backstage – these usually contain outlets for lighting instruments – or on the stage – these usually contain outlets for sound equipment. Both typically also contain an Edison* outlet.

FLOWN vs. TRAVELED
The terms traveling and flying usually pertain to a drape* that goes across the full stage, such as the main* or the mid-traveler*. Most of these drapes hang from a pipe, and also have curtain pulls like a curtain in your home. So, when the pipe is lifted vertically this is called flying, or that the drape or set piece is flown. When the curtain is flown in such that the bottom is touching the stage deck* then when you pull the curtain ropes to open the curtain horizontally, half to the left, half to the right, then this is known as traveling.

FLYING
You may think of Peter Pan when you think of "flying", however in the case of technical theatre "flying" is what the flyman* does. It refers to moving the hung scenery* and lighting instruments* in* and out* of the stage space. A crew member may be told to "fly* in* that flat*".

FLYMAN
This term refers to the person (male or female) who operates the fly system*/counterweight system*/rigging* during a show.

FLY RAIL or LOCKING RAIL or RAIL
The fly rail/locking rail/rail is generally referred to as the area where the ropes of a fly system*/counterweight system*/rigging* are located. A flyman* is said to be "working on the rail". Specifically it refers to the length of metal railing where the rope locks are affixed.

FLY ROPE
This is the actual rope used in a fly system*/counterweight system*/rigging* system. It has properties that allow it to carry hundreds of pounds of weight. It is the part of the system that the flyman* pulls in order to move the scenery*.

FLY SYSTEM or COUNTERWEIGHT SYSTEM or RIGGING
This is the system of ropes that you typically see back stage in a theatre. The term "counterweight" comes from the fact that the scenery* or lighting instruments* are in some way counter weighted so that the weights on one end of the ropes weigh as much as the scenery* or lighting instruments* on the pipes, so that they are easy for one person to move in* and out*. These days it's most common to find pig irons* providing the counterweights, however some theatres still use sand bags. Some rigging systems use winches, which can adjust to the weight of the scenery* or lighting instruments*, and do not require physical re-weighting by technicians*.

FLY TOWER
This is the tallest part of your theatre building. It houses the counterweight* system, and allows lighting instruments* and scenery* to be pulled up out of sight of the audience. Many high schools opt to have a ¾ fly tower. This not only saves money in construction materials, but in a ¾ fly tower the proscenium* opening is smaller and therefore a fire curtain is not required. The curse of a ¾ fly tower is that the scenery cannot fully be pulled out of sight of the audience and there is usually a few inches that hang down below the sight lines, and when the scenery is flown in often times the pipe it is hanging from is visible. Another drawback to a ¾ fly is that the grid is flush up against the ceiling, instead of being about 6' below it, so access to the cables of the counterweight* system is limited in case a repair is needed.

FOCUS
Focusing the lights is the process whereby the lighting technicians* aim the lighting instruments* in the correct position and in the correct format as decided by the lighting designer, in order for them to fulfill the purpose for which they were intended.

FOLLOWSPOT
The followspot, or spot light as some Muggles* call it, is a large lighting instrument* usually mounted on a pole at chest-height, that can be moved around by an operator. The purpose of the followspot is to highlight a specific performer, usually

a main character during a song of a musical or possibly a stand-up comedian alone on the stage. Because the performer moves around the stage the followspot operator can "follow" the movement and "spot" the performer with the light*.

GAFF TAPE
This tape is as wide as duct tape and is usually black (it comes in other colors, but black is the most practical for the theatre). It is used in the theatre for all sorts of uses, including securing items and cables. This tapes lifts off fairly easily and doesn't leave a sticky mess. NEVER use duct tape in the theatre.

GALLERY
This is a recessed walkway along the side of a house* that allows for lighting instruments* to be hung, which are easily accessible. There can be one, two or three levels. It's also a favorite place for directors to want to place performers.

GARAGE DOOR
As the name suggest – unlike most things in a theatre – a garage door is like a garage door; just not in a garage. It is a large roll-up door, usually made of metal, that is tall enough and wide enough to move large pieces of scenery* through. There is usually a garage door from the scene shop* to the loading dock of the theatre, and another garage door from the scene shop to the backstage hallway, and then another garage door from the backstage hallway to backstage. Some theatres that have their scene shop directly behind the backstage wall (not recommended!) have the garage door leading directly from the scene shop to backstage.

GEL
This is the colored filter that is put in front of a lighting instrument and held in place by a gel frame*. Gels actually used to be made of gelatin, which is how they got their name. They held up ok under the hot lighting instruments*, but if you put them in water they were reduced to a soggy mess. These days gels are synthetically made of a type of polyester. There are hundreds and hundreds of gel colors, each one varying slightly from the next – and yet Lighting Designers complain there are never enough colors.

GEL FRAME
This is the metal frame that holds a square of gel* in place in front of the lighting instrument*. There is a slot in the front of the lighting instrument* where the gel frame slides into.

GENIE
Not the kind that comes out of a lamp or bottle. If there were that kind of genies in theatres, technicians' jobs would be obsolete. So we don't allow them. But we welcome "genie lifts", which are scissor, or vertical mast lifts that allows a technician to work high in the air – usually above 20' in order to work on a set* piece or to focus lighting instruments*. "Genie" is actually a brand name, but in the theatre "genie" has become a common term for any lift, much like a "Kleenex" can refer to any tissue.

GHOST LIGHT or NIGHT LIGHT
This is the light that is typically left on when a theatre is unoccupied. It is so that the first person next entering the theatre can see in order to reach the switches for the worklights. The theatre is a very dangerous place, and not somewhere that someone should be walking around in in the pitch black. Night lights are sometimes traditionally called ghosts lights, so that there is some light left of for the traditional theatre ghost to see by. The night light can be just a lamp on a stand that is wheeled out to center-stage and plugged in, or it can be a fixture hardwired into a lighting system and usually situated in the beams* or catwalks*

GLOW TAPE
When activated by bright light, this tape glows in the dark. It is primarily used backstage* (sometimes on stage) at the edge of platforms, stairs, etc, so that actors, crew* and techs* can see the edge and don't trip and fall during a black out. Glow tape is very expensive and should be used sparingly.

GOBO
This refers to a pattern that is inserted into a lighting instrument*. It can be made of metal, glass or can be a photographic image much like a slide. Metal gobos can be "break up patterns" which looks like dappled light coming through trees, to more specific shapes such as a window, a castle, snowflakes, and so on. Glass gobos can be used to create fire and water effects.

GP
GP stands for General Purpose, and is a pipe* that is not designated to hold lighting instruments* or clouds*. GPs are typically used for hanging scenery* on.

GRAND or MAIN
This is the large curtain that hangs just upstage* of the proscenium arch*. It is the curtain that separates the stage from the house*, the actor from the audience. It is commonly referred to as just the "main" or the "grand".

HANDHELD
This is a shortened term for a handheld wireless microphone*.

HANG AND FOCUS
This is the term used for the process whereby the technicians* hang the lighting instruments* in the positions where the lighting designer determines where they need to go, patches* where the lights are plugged in into the light board and then focuses* the instruments* for the correct function.

HEADSET
You will hear of two types of headsets spoken about around a theatre. One type belongs to the theatre's communication system that the crew uses and the other kind are mics* that performers wear. Usually if you just hear the term "headset" used by itself we are talking about the communication system. Also, you will hear the whole arrangement, which includes the headset, beltpack and cables referred

to as "the headset". Technically the beltpack carries the power and the headset itself is plugged into it, but we call the whole thing "the headset". When a Stage Manager tells her crew to "set up the headsets" she means to plug in or put in place the headsets, cables and beltpacks.

HOUSE
The house is where the audience sits.

HOUSELIGHTS
These are the fixtures that light up the house*. In a full theatre they are on dimmers so that they can be adjusted slowly or partially.

IN, OUT, ON, OFF
In the theatre you fly pipes* "in" (down) and "out" (up), and you move scenery or actors "on" (into the view of the audience) and "off" (away from the view of the audience).

INSTRUMENTS
This primarily refers to the lighting instruments. Instruments are movable – usually installed on a pipe* with a C-Clamp. As opposed to fixtures that are the lighting fixtures you would find in your house or office – these are hardwired in or "fixed".

LADDERS
In this case the ladders don't refer to the things you climb, but the lighting pipes and raceways that hang on either side of the stage in more recently built theatres. These allow for side lighting, especially important in dance (in order to light the whole body, not just the face). Most theatres that have light ladders have one upstage* of each leg*, and there are usually 3 or 6 instruments on each ladder.

LAMP
"It's called a *lamp*!" is a favorite theatre cry. Never a "light bulb". The "bulb" is just the glass part. A "lamp" is made of the bulb, a filament, the gas and a base.

LLAMA
An example of live animals that are often not permitted in theatres. Not only do live animals draw attention away from the actors, but their behavior can be unpredictable. They can poop, throw up and spit. If you have a tens of thousands of dollars of drapes on your stage, you may wish to consider animals carefully. Animals can also "freak out" and run or fall into the audience, risking harming themselves and the audience. Allow the use of llamas or any live animals at your peril.

LEGS
These are the narrow (usually black) drapes that hang on either side of the stage. They are usually parallel to the front edge of the stage, sometimes they are angled slightly. These serve to hide the view of backstage* from the audience, yet allow performers to enter and exit the stage at various places. They also allow set pieces to be moved on and off stage, without the audience seeing them being stored off-stage*, and also allow for the stage to be lit from the side.

LIGHT
The stuff that comes out of a lamp.

LOBBY
The area where the audience waits to be let into the house*. Concessions* are usually sold in the lobby.

LOCKING RAIL or FLY RAIL or RAIL
The fly rail/locking rail/rail is generally referred to as the area where the ropes of a fly system*/counterweight system*/rigging* are located. A flyman* is said to be "working on the rail". Specifically it refers to the length of metal railing where the rope locks are affixed.

MAIN or GRAND
This is the large curtain that hangs just upstage* of the proscenium arch*. It is the curtain that separates the stage from the house*, the actor from the audience. It is commonly referred to as just the "main" or the "grand".

MAINSTAGE
In a performing arts center that has more than one theatre, the main stage refers to the largest theatre. The main stage is usually a proscenium* theatre, while a second theatre is usually black box* theatre.

MARLEY
This is a "rubber"-like floor that is laid down over the stage deck* for dancers. It usually comes in long strips about 6' x 40'. The strips are taped together with marley tape.

MASKING
The masking refers to a drape* - usually a black drape* - that masks the audience's view to the backstage* area. This is usually the legs*, mid-traveler*, side masking and upstage* masking.

MIC
Short for microphone. There are several types of mics, the most common being the vocal mic, the instrument mic, the condenser mic, the floor or plate mic, and the wireless handheld mic. Each type of mic has a different polar pattern*.

MID-TRAVELER
The mid-traveler, as the name suggests is a drape that usually hangs in the middle of the stage*, and travels* open and closed, although it can also be flown*.

MONITOR (SOUND)
When a part of a sound system, this refers to a speaker that is placed on stage or in the pit so that the performers can hear music or other performers that are usually hard to hear from where you are. For instance, dancers on a stage find it hard to hear music coming from speakers that are only in the house*, and orchestra

members in the pit* find it hard to hear the actors' lines from up on the stage. Usually just the word "monitor" is used and the specific item is inferred from the context of the conversation.

MONITOR (A/V)
When backstage* this refers to a video screen in a dressing room or classroom that is hooked up to a camera in the house* that is aimed at the stage. This is so that performers can be watching what is going on on stage, so that they know when to enter, without being in the way backstage*. Usually just the word "monitor" is used and the specific item is inferred from the context of the conversation.

MUGGLE
What's a Muggle? According to Dictionary.com, a "muggle" is a term originating from around the 1920's to describe a person "*who is ignorant or has no skills*". Oxforddictionaries.com defines a Muggle as "*A person who is not conversant with a particular activity or skill*". Both refer to the meaning popularized in the Harry Potter series: "a person without magical powers". In the theatre, where we create the "magic", a Muggle good-naturedly refers to a non-'theatre person' who does not have a knowledge of what goes on behind the scenes in order to make the "magic of theatre" happen.

NIGHT LIGHT or GHOST LIGHT
This is the light that is typically left on when a theatre is unoccupied. It is so that the first person next entering the theatre can see in order to reach the switches for the worklights. The theatre is a very dangerous place, and not somewhere that someone should be walking around in in the pitch black. Night lights are sometimes traditionally called ghosts lights, so that there is some light left of for the traditional theatre ghost to see by. The night light can be just a lamp on a stand that is wheeled out to center-stage and plugged in, or it can be a fixture hardwired into a lighting system and usually situated in the beams* or catwalks*

OFF-STAGE
This refers to the part of the stage deck* that is hidden behind the drapes* or masking* - the part that the audience can't see. It is also a directional command – the actor walks "off-stage".

PAC
Performing Arts Center. This term interchangeably refers to the whole building housing the theatre (house* and stage) and classrooms, or just the theatre itself. The meaning can be found in the context of the conversation.

PATCH
Patching is a lighting and a sound term. Instead of the first fader on the light or sound board, for instance, controlling the first circuit where the lighting instrument* or mic* is plugged in, the technician may prefer for the first fader to control a lighting instrument* or mic* that is operating in a certain area of the stage. So the technician will patch the appropriate instrument* or mic* into an appropriate fader. A similar concept to old patch boards that telephone operators used to control.

PIG IRONS
Pig irons are the metal weights that are used to counter balance the scenery* or lighting pipes* so that they can easily be flown in* or out*. There are three general sizes (or weights), the larger is fondly called a Pig, the next is called a Half-pig, and the smallest are called Piglets. Some people call them "bricks" instead, as they look somewhat like bricks.

PIPES or BATTENS
The pipes that hang above the stage and hold lights, mics and scenery. The pipes that hold the lights are called Electrics* and the pipes available for scenery hanging are called GPs*. Another common pipe is the Cloud Truss*.

PIT
The pit refers to the orchestra pit, which is a large space in front of the stage and usually about 8 or so feet below the stage deck* level. This is so that the orchestra can play and be heard, but not block the view of the stage from the house*. During shows when there is no orchestra, the pit is usually covered up with a pit cover, which looks like an extension of the stage deck*.

POLAR PATTERN
This refers to the direction from a mic* picks up sound. Some pick up sound from only one direction (uni-directional) and some pick up sound from more than one direction (bi-directional).

PRODUCTION LIGHTS
Production lights refer to what most people think of as "stage lights". They are the lights that are used during a performance. As opposed to work lights* which are used for rehearsals, classes and for technical purposes.

PROP
This is any item that a performer carries on stage with them. Anything else – such as a chair or picture frame – is considered a set* piece.

PROSCENIUM or PROSCENUIM ARCH
The proscenium arch is the opening in the front wall of the house*, which frames the stage.

RACEWAY
This is the long 'box' with circuits that runs along a lighting pipe or electric*, into which the lighting instruments are plugged.

RAIL or LOCKING RAIL or FLY RAIL
The fly rail/locking rail/rail is generally referred to as the area where the ropes of a fly system*/counterweight system*/rigging* are located. A flyman* is said to be "working on the rail". Specifically it refers to the length of metal railing where the rope locks are affixed.

RAKE STAGE or RAKED STAGE
A raked stage is a stage that is angled. The front of the stage (literally downstage*) is lower than the back of the stage (literally upstage*).

RE-WEIGHTING
This is the process whereby the weights on a counterweight system* are either added or removed in order to match the weight of the scenery* or lighting instruments* added or removed from a batten*.

RIDER
This is a document from an event coming into the theatre that instructs the theatre technicians* what technical requirements they will have for the event.

RIGGING or COUNTERWEIGHT SYSTEM or FLY SYSTEM
This is the system of ropes that you typically see back stage in a theatre. It is also called the counterweight system* or the fly system*.

RISERS
The steps that a choir stands on so that you can see all performers and so that all performers voices can be projected.

RUN THROUGH
A run through is when the cast rehearses the whole play in one go, instead of just focusing on particular scenes or acts.

RUNNING ORDER
This is a list of what happens when in a show – such as for a variety show, the Running Order might start: M.C. welcomes audience, dance #1, song #1, M.C. talks, dance #2, skit #1, and so on. All technicians* need to have a copy of the Running Order of a show that they are rehearsing so that they can make notes about what they need to do for the performance.

SCENE SHOP
This is the room backstage where the sets* are built, painted and stored.

SCENERY or SET
A piece of scenery or a set* piece refers to an item on stage that a performer does not carry or move – as opposed to a prop* - such as a wall, stairs, a tree and so on.

SET or SCENERY
A set piece or piece of scenery* refers to an item on stage that a performer does not carry or move – as opposed to a prop* - such as a wall, stairs, a tree and so on.

SHELLS
Shells are movable walls that can be place behind musicians so that the sound is better bounced into the audience. It helps the audience better hear a group of instrumental or vocal musicians, while a mic* helps the audience hear a specific musician.

SHOP
A shop in the theatre is the place where items are built and stored.

STAGE MANAGER (SM)
The Stage Manager is the person in charge of the smooth running order* of a performance. While each technician* knows what their job is for any specific cue*, the SM makes sure that all of the cues* happen at the right time.

SOFT GOODS
This refers to any of the drapes* in a theatre.

SPIKE
To spike something means to place a small piece of spike tape* on the stage deck* to indicate where the item should be placed. For instance, during a set change a technician* may have to set a table exactly where a focused* lighting instrument* will hit it during a following scene. In order to be sure to place the table in the same location night after night the table is spiked. Another thing that is spiked can be the ropes of the counterweight* system. Often times a technician* pulling the ropes during a performance may not be able to see when to stop, so the rope is spiked at the location where the set* piece is in place. In either case, this is called being "on spike".

SPIKE TAPE
Spike tape is a special type of tape used to spike* the set or ropes. It is fairly thin, comes in a variety of colors and is easily removable once the show it done (almost nothing created in the theatre is permanent). The different colors are useful to spike* the set* pieces for different scenes – for instance, the furniture locations for scene one can be done in green spike tape and the furniture locations for the second scene can be done in orange spike tape, in order to not cause confusion as to what needs to be placed where and when.

STAGE LEFT
This is from the actor's perspective. If you are sitting in the house watching a show, stage left would be on your right.

STAGE PIN or THREE PRONG TWIST or EDISON
These are the there most common types of lighting instrument* plugs and outlets that you will find in the theatre. Edison refers to your standard household plug. Stage pin also has three pins or prongs, but they are in alignment. Three prong twist has three pins or prongs that form a circle, one prong has a tab and once the plug is inserted into the outlet it is twisted to secure it.

STAGE RIGHT
This is from the actor's perspective. If you are sitting in the house watching a show, stage right would be on your left.

STANDBY
When a Stage Manager* calls a standby it is to alert the technicians* that they have a cue* coming up. Typically once an SM* calls a standby no one must talk over the headsets* until the cue* is complete, because the timing of the cues* can be essential and the technicians* need to hear the SM say "Go."

STRIKE
This term refers to the taking down, dismantling disposing, and/or storage of the set, lights, sound equipment and costumes once a show is over. Some plays will strike after the closing night performance, which can take into the wee hours. In educational theatre, students aren't allowed to stay up that late, so some pieces may be struck on closing night, but the majority of the strike will happen the next day.

TECH REHEARSAL
This refers to the final rehearsals prior to opening night where the technical aspects are integrated into the show. Prior to tech rehearsals the actors will have been rehearsing with minimal costumes and props*, and perhaps just large blocks or classroom chairs as set pieces. They also do not have lighting cues* or use mics*. The tech rehearsals are for the actors to get used to working with all of the technical aspects of the show and for the technicians* to have a chance to "rehearse" their parts – such as when does a light cue happen and when does a set piece have to move. Tech rehearsals can be boring for the actors who have been used to running their show non-stop by that time, while the technicians* move at a slower pace as they record their cues*, sort out any problems and get used to their jobs.

TECHNICIAN, TECH, TECHIE or TECH CREW
This refers to a person who helps with the technical, non-acting, side of a show. Good technicians are never noticed by an audience.

THREE PRONG TWIST or EDISON or STAGE PIN
These are the there most common types of lighting instrument* plugs and outlets that you will find in the theatre. Edison refers to your standard household plug. Stage pin also has three pins or prongs, but they are in alignment. Three prong twist has three pins or prongs that form a circle, one prong has a tab and once the plug is inserted into the outlet it is twisted to secure it.

THRUST STAGE
A thrust stage is a stage with audience members on three sides – the stage "thrusts" into the audience.

THEATRE-IN-THE-ROUND
Theatre-in-the-round is where the audience surrounds the stage on all sides. Despite the name "round" this is usually a square stage.

TICKET BOOTH
Most people are familiar with this term because most people have been to a production or sporting event where they've had to purchase or pick up tickets from the ticket booth. Some theatres use their ticket booths solely for that reason, and some ticket booths also do double duty as an office. This is not to be confused with the term Booth*, which is used by itself.

TRAVELED vs. FLOWN
The terms traveling and flying usually pertain to a drape* that goes across the full stage, such as the main* or the mid-traveler*. Most of these drapes hang from a pipe, and also have curtain pulls like a curtain in your home. So, when the pipe is lifted vertically this is called flying, or that the drape or set piece is flown. When the curtain is flown in such that the bottom is touching the stage deck* then when you pull the curtain ropes to open the curtain horizontally, half to the left, half to the right, then this is known as traveling.

TWO-FERS
Two-fers are a Y shaped lighting cables that allow two instruments to be plugged into one outlet. Two "fer" one. Very useful in a theatre that doesn't have enough circuits.

UPSTAGE
Most people have no trouble remembering stage left* and stage right* as being from the actor's perspective, however remembering which is upstage and downstage* is harder. Downstage is towards the audience and upstage is towards the back wall of the stage. Here's how to remember: These days our stages are usually, mostly level, while the house* is raked*. In Shakespearean times the floor where the audience stood or sat was level, while the stage was raked. So when the actors walked towards the audience, they were literally walking down hill (down the stage) and when the actors walked away from the audience, towards the back wall of the stage, they were literally walking up hill (up the stage). Hence the terms upstage and downstage.

USHER
An usher is a person who takes tickets and helps audience members find their seats.

WINGS
This refers to the space backstage* from the legs* or masking* to the backstage* wall. The wings traditionally refers to just the sides of the backstage* space, hence the term "waiting in the wings".

WINCH
An electric winch can be used instead of a counterweight* system. Winches can automatically adjust to hundreds of pounds of weight without the need for the

technician* to re-weight*. The pipes are then moved by pressing a button instead of pulling on a rope.

WIRELESS MIC
A mic that transmits a signal to a receiver which then relays the information to the sound board, as oppose to being wired into the system and then physically patched* into the sound board.

WORK LIGHTS
These are lights that are to be used anytime someone needs to be in the theatre for any reason, other than there being a show in progress. In that case, Production Lights* are used. Work Lights are always a white light, and are usually mounted on the electrics*, the beams* and/or the side walls of the stage.
A word about Work Lights. Some theatres have been known to use their Production Lights* because they have no Work Lights. Consider this – if all of the Production Lights are on, that adds up to about 120,000watts of power used, not to mention the replacement cost of the lamps and gels that are being burned through. LEDs are the best Work Lights because they are energy saving, have a long lamp life and turn on and off immediately. HIDs also save energy and have a long lamp life, but take about 10 minutes to warm up, and if you turn them off and then need them on again immediately they can take up to 20 minutes to warm back up again (this is another common reason for people turning on Production Lights – impatience). Fluorescents have a longer lamp life than Production Lights, but a much shorter lamp life than LEDs and HIDs. It is worth the money to get work lights installed if you don't have them, and worth your effort to insist they're used if you do have them.

Made in the USA
San Bernardino, CA
16 July 2015